THE TRUTH IS OUT THERE

THE TRUTH IS OUT THERE

The Ultimate World Conspiracy
Who Really *Is* Pulling the Strings?

Steve Maltz

Authentic

MILTON KEYNES ● COLORADO SPRINGS ● HYDERABAD

14 13 12 11 10 09 08   8 7 6 5 4 3 2

Reprinted 2008

Authentic Media, 9 Holdom Avenue, Bletchley, Milton Keynes,
Bucks., MK1 1QR
1820 Jet Stream Drive, Colorado Springs, CO 80921, USA
OM Authentic Media, Medchal Road, Jeedimetla Village,
Secunderabad 500 055, A.P., India
www.authenticmedia.co.uk
Authentic Media is a division of IBS-STL U.K., limited by
guarantee, with its registered office at Kingstown Broadway,
Carlisle, Cumbria CA3 0HA. Registered in England & Wales
No.1216232. Registered charity 270162

British Library Cataloguing in Publication Data

A catalogue record for this book is available from the
British Library

ISBN-13: 978-1-86024-573-2
ISBN-10: 1-86204-573-0

Cover Design by fourninezero design.
Print Management by Adare Carwin
Printed in Great Britain by J.H. Haynes & Co., Sparkford

Contents

	Introduction	ix
	Prologue	xiii
1.	Starry, Starry Night	1
2.	The End is Nigh	11
3.	Life, Just as We Know it	21
4.	It's All in the Design	32
5.	Our Darkest Hour	43
6.	The Eye of the Beholder	50
7.	Ghosts in the Machine	57
8.	From David Beckham to Little Green Men	65
9.	Unexpected Impossibilities	73
10.	That Still, Small Voice	80
	And Finally	87
	Recommended Reading	95

Contents

Introduction

1. ...

2. ...

To the unknown searcher

INTRODUCTION

Look at the success of *The Da Vinci Code* in this decade, *Chariots of the Gods* in the 1960s, or *The Late Great Planet Earth* in the 1970s. We love intrigues and mysteries, especially when there is a blurring between truth and fiction. If a major event occurs that contains just the slightest whiff of uncertainty or controversy, watch as the conspiracy industry buds some new shoots. Some, such as the Kennedy assassination, 9/11 and the death of Princess Diana, have become mighty oaks. Others, long forgotten, have just withered and died, denied the oxygen of media attention.

Conspiracies are big news. The media industry loves them because we love them, though there's a touch of 'the chicken or egg' here – would we be bothered to see the death of Princess Diana as anything other than an accident statistic if it weren't for Al Fayed's insistence of a cover-up and the acres of newsprint churned out in commentary and speculation? On the other hand there is something gloriously perverse in believing negative stories about the British Royal Family. It is both empowering and intriguing and lifts us out of our mundane lives into the twilight world of spies and assassins. Does it matter if there's every possibility that there's not a scrap of truth in it? Why spoil a thumping good read?

Some conspiracy theories go deeper. Rather than being sparked off by a single event, they speak of shadowy organizations that have been pulling the strings of history from the year dot. These speculations have been with us ever since the birth of the gossip column (about two days after the invention of the printing press) and have created an industry of cosmic tittle-tattle, with myriad websites, millionaire authors and a worldwide network feeding the hungry masses.

If there is one central theme that occurs again and again it is this: who really controls the world? Many have been suggested as prime candidates. There are the secret societies of the Freemasons, the Rosicrucians, the Bilderberg Group, the Illuminati, the New World Order. There are the Rothschilds and the Rockefellers. There are even the veiled lizards of David Icke, ex-BBC snooker commentator and now full-time 'messiah'. There are the Jews and the Catholics, favourite scapegoats for those who are neither. Welcome on board the Paranoia Express, standing room only!

Are we throwing the baby out with the bathwater if we dismiss them all as the fruit of overactive or disturbed minds? Can there be elements of truth in some of these theories, with the secret being how to find the right mix? After all, there are the usual suspects, such as the Royal Family, the Bush family and Henry Kissinger, who crop up in a number of them. Is it just a case of finding a key that fits all the locks? Or is there a deeper conspiracy, concerned not with the machinations of individuals with agendas, but with unseen powers and forces lurking just out of view?

Just as the scientists work towards finding the 'Theory of Everything' that would explain the currently unexplainable, conspiracy theorists must surely, deep down, hanker for the real truth at the heart of our complicated world. Is history just a random sequence of events, or are there secret manipulations? What makes us tick? How did the world as we see it come to be? Is it fair to expect answers, or is it folly not to be asking the questions in the first place?

In this short book we will be delving below the surface of our existence on this planet, glimpsing the possibilities beyond the daily routines of simply getting on with life. Of course you may be quite happy with your lot, but there's surely no harm in having your brain cells tickled and your soul (or whatever it is that is you) challenged. By doing so we will be discovering that perhaps there is something going on out there, perhaps even a conspiracy of sorts.

Our conspiracy has tentacles in all spheres of human life, so where it leads we will follow. It will take us into areas of science, history, human behaviour, popular culture and religion. It's a small book, so we will do little more than dip into each, just enough to tickle the palate. If it awakes a thirst, recommendations are made for further reading, putting you in the hands of experts who will take you further.

Of course, the very word conspiracy implies dastardly deeds, selfish ambitions and world domination, so we must tread carefully. Just be true to yourself and be prepared to evaluate not only all that you read here, but also all that you have read before.

'*Truth is more of a stranger than fiction.*' Mark Twain.

PROLOGUE

The press had called it E-day. It was a unique event, not seen in Britain for over seventy years, and it was going to happen over Cornwall on 11 August 1999 at around 11 a.m. It was, of course, a total eclipse of the Sun and I was ready for it, in the Lake District, around six hundred miles north of ground zero, but still with a reasonable view. As it turned out, most of Cornwall was in cloud when it happened, but we had a good view on Brant Fell, just outside Bowness, by Windermere. Smug in the thought that a 90 per cent eclipse in clear sky over the Lakes was better than a 100 per cent eclipse lost in the Cornish clouds, I stood with my family, plastic dark glasses (courtesy of a tabloid newspaper) and pin-hole projection device made from a cereal box at the ready. It didn't disappoint. We got our cosmic performance, ooh-ed and aah-ed for a few minutes, then followed the sated crowd back into town for lunch.

We tend to take such things for granted, an entertainment to slot alongside the CGI-laden movies and technical wizardry of sci-fi dramas on the TV. Yet this was no illusion brought about through the manipulation of photons by indulged technicians; this was real life, a mother nature production and free!

However, if we only realized it, a total eclipse is a completely unlikely event. Patrick Moore, that monocled eccentric (and probably the finest amateur astronomer of modern times), calls it 'unquestionably the finest display in all Nature',[1] but he also says that the fact that it happens at all is 'pure chance'.

A total eclipse of the Sun only occurs because, from our perspective as we peer at the skies, the Sun and Moon seem to be about the same size, so that when the Moon passes exactly in front of the Sun, it blots it out to our eyes – the ultimate sunblock. It's simple really. There's nothing magical about that if, indeed, the Sun and Moon are the same size. But they are not. The Sun is around four hundred times larger than the Moon and the only reason they seem to be the same size is that the Sun is around four hundred times further away from us. If the Moon was 5 per cent smaller or larger or the Sun was 5 per cent smaller or larger, there could never be a total eclipse. Nor could there be if the Moon or Sun were 5 per cent nearer or further away. It's a fine balance here: a slight nudge either way would deprive us of this 'finest display in all Nature'.

So what, you may ask. After all, eclipses have had a bad press in earlier days. They have generally been seen as portents of doom. Not surprising really, as you wouldn't expect to see a dark, star-lit sky in the middle of the day unless something dastardly was about to happen. That was the thinking in earlier times, when the phenomenon was seen as the Sun abandoning the Earth, usually as a result of being gulped down by a dragon or a demon. The ancient Chinese used to bang drums to frighten away the dragon. The Incas used to fire arrows at the sky. Of course, they were successful: the Sun was rescued as the eclipse finished. They had no reason to believe otherwise.

Then the scientists came along to tell us that it's not the work of angry gods or demons, but rather a trick of geometry. This inclines us to think that maybe we are better off without such natural phenomena, but something still nags at me.

'The finest display in all Nature'. Surely this is reason enough to enjoy it and qualify it as one of life's more meaningful experiences.

Only if such things matter to you, of course, otherwise we just shrug our shoulders, mutter 'seen that, done that,' and carve a fresh notch on our personal bedpost of life. It may not seem important to you, but surely it's worth a brief consideration. To the scientific community, total eclipses have a further importance. In fact a whole scientific discipline, star astrophysics, was developed in the late nineteenth century simply out of the data that can be obtained by observing the Sun's surface during a total eclipse. Also, data produced at the 1919 eclipse helped to verify Albert Einstein's general theory of relativity. So it's not just touchy-feely stuff here; we're also looking at the cold world of hard facts benefiting from the 'amazing coincidence' of factors working together to produce this phenomenon.

I've always wanted to see the Aurora Borealis, but live too far south ever to have witnessed it. Of course, that's why they are called the 'Northern Lights'. Yet my brain tells me that it's just an atmospheric effect caused by the solar wind, an accident of optics just as the eclipse is an accident of geometry. But my heart tells me otherwise and convinces me that there are some things in life worth experiencing just for what they are, as if they have been put in our world for that very purpose. Things that draw us out of our humdrum lives and fill us with wonder. And if such things as a total eclipse of the Sun are so improbable that their very existence hangs on a thread, statistically speaking, then we should appreciate them even more.

This book nudges us to consider such things as eclipses and the Aurora Borealis. To get to the heart of what is going on in the world, we must use all our senses. We are not just brains on legs; there's more to us than that. Perhaps thinking deeper about this thing called the eclipse is a good place to start . . .

Notes

[1] Patrick Moore, *The Amateur Astronomer* (Cambridge: Lutterworth Press, 1957), p. 85.

CHAPTER 1

STARRY, STARRY NIGHT

You've got to admit it is a bit weird, now that you've had time to take in the facts. If the Moon or Sun were just a tiny bit smaller or larger or nearer or farther away, there could never be total eclipses of the Sun.

It's not just about entertainment, though. It's not simply a matter of having something beautiful to look at. It seems that the Sun and the Moon are the size and distance away that they are for a far more important reason. If they weren't just as they are, life on Earth would not be. We would not exist, or at best we'd live as scraps of amoeba or bacteria. If we were 5 per cent closer to the Sun we would burn to a crisp in a runaway greenhouse effect. If we were a tad further away from the Sun, we would suffocate in a cloud of carbon dioxide. If the Moon were a little larger, our tides would swamp the Earth. If it were smaller, there would be no tides at all.

But it doesn't end there. When you look at our Solar System as a whole, all nine planets with their collection of moons, there is another amazing fact. It appears that out of these seventy heavenly bodies, the surface of the Earth is the *only* place in the whole Solar System where a total eclipse can be seen properly (leaving aside the

1

obvious fact that standing on the surface of any of these other places would either vaporize you or freeze you solid). So the focus is not just on the Sun and the Moon but on the Earth itself.

And what about the Earth? In ancient days the Earth was considered the centre of the universe. The clever term is 'geocentric'. One of the first thinkers to come up with this idea was Pythagoras (of the square on the hypotenuse fame). He suggested that the Sun, Moon and five nearest planets all spun round the Earth in perfect circles. This remained popular for some time as it spoke of a stationary Earth, with the rest of the heavenly bodies moving round it. The religious establishment, whether the Ancient Greeks or the medieval church, liked this, as it put Earth and humankind at the centre of things. The alternative view of the Earth moving round the Sun was considered not just heresy but ridiculous: if the Earth moved we'd feel it, wouldn't we?

But along came a Polish astronomer, Copernicus, who turned this on its head. He proved that the Earth did, indeed, move round the Sun, as did the other planets. The term for this is 'heliocentric'. What was significant about this development, however, was something deeper than mere scientific speculation. It directly challenged received wisdom. It implied that despite what the Bible and the ancient philosophers seemed to be saying, the Earth was nothing special in the great scheme of things. It was called the Copernican Principle, or the Mediocrity Principle, and confined us to living on a mediocre planet, orbiting a mediocre star in a mediocre galaxy.

This has remained the favoured view of scientists and philosophers ever since. They like to see the universe as one vast democracy, with equal voting rights for all the planets, stars, black holes and what have you. No favouritism in boffin-land. To them, the title 'third rock from the Sun' just about sums us up. Nothing special, nothing remarkable: that's us.

But there's a conspiracy afoot and it's not a conspiracy of silence. It's like no conspiracy you've ever heard of, as it exists for no selfish purpose. It's not about power, greed or ambition; it's about possibilities and purpose. It's a *benign* conspiracy; it's there for your benefit, whether you know it or not. It works mainly in the background and most are unaware of its existence. But it is there and it works on your behalf, drawing to itself those who thirst for a life of meaning and purpose. It tells you to engage your brain and think for yourself.

We have a brain in our head, with the capacity for rational thought. We have a heart beating in our chest, with the desire for passionate inquiry. Was Copernicus right, or is there something special about Earth? Many scientists are now beginning to ask this question and most of them are not religious nuts. So why are they asking it?

They are doing so because of the rapid advances in scientific knowledge in modern times, particularly in the new ways that things around us can be observed, measured and evaluated. Scientists have discovered some remarkable things. Taken alone they would just be considered quirks or oddities, but taken together – and there's an awfully large number of them – they tell an awesome story.

We'll start with the facts already considered, matters of geography. First we consider the distance between the Earth and the Sun. If you want life to occur on any planet, it must be within a certain distance of the Sun, in the space called the habitable zone. It must be not so near that the water in the oceans boils away, and not so far away that it freezes over. Earth is the only planet within that zone.

The Sun itself, one of the largest stars around, is just the perfect size for life on Earth. If it had been any smaller, Earth would have had to be closer to it in order to stay warm enough for life, and this would have created separate problems with rotation, meaning that one side of the Earth could have been permanently cold and the other burning hot, as is the case with the planet Mercury.

Then there's the Moon to consider. The size of the Moon and its distance from the Earth are also critical. They have to be just right to control the tilt of the Earth and to create suitable climates on Earth for life to flourish.

So the relationship between the Sun, the Earth and the Moon is just right to support life on Earth. That's fine, but then the universe is a vast space and surely there can be other Earths out there with the same relationships. There's every possibility, of course.

Moving outwards into the Solar System, we discover that Jupiter, the largest planet, is in just the right orbit round the Sun to act as protector of Earth, by capturing asteroids and comets which otherwise could threaten to knock lumps out of us.

As for the Earth itself, scientists have discovered how finely tuned it is in so many ways. The magnetic field is just right, the amount of oxygen in the atmosphere is just right, the rate of rotation is just right, the size and properties of the Earth's crust are just right. The list goes on and, in fact, scientists have come up with a list of twenty things that need to be just right: if any one of them were slightly different, life on Earth just wouldn't be.

It gets interesting when we consider that for any other planet out there in the universe to be suitable for life, it too would need to have all these things in place. You begin to wonder.

The year was 1973. A group of scientists had gathered in Krakow, Poland, to commemorate the 500th birthday of Copernicus, the man whose discoveries, as we remember, led to the labelling of the Earth as a mediocre planet in a nobody Solar System in a second-rate galaxy. The title of the conference was 'Confrontation of Cosmological Theories with Observational Data'.[1]

A British physicist, Brandon Carter, made a startling proclamation that went against the grain of all that this gathering stood for. He stated that he had come to the conclusion that despite the common views arising from Copernican thinking, the Earth was indeed very special and humanity did indeed hold a special place in the universe. How ironic: surely Copernicus turned in his grave at such an affront.

Carter was the first to voice an uncomfortable new theory, the Anthropic Principle. In its simplest terms it states that the whole universe seems to be constructed in such a way as to make life possible. To Carter it seemed that by our very existence as intelligent creatures, we impose a sort of selection effect on the universe, in that if the universe were even slightly different, we wouldn't be here to observe it. The universe appears to have been specifically designed for the existence and well-being of human beings. In fact all evidence seems to point to a true benign conspiracy.

This was an earth-shattering theory and controversial, but it wasn't without substance. Suddenly the Earth was special again; suddenly we were special again. It seemed that the universe was 'fine-tuned' to allow the existence of life as we know it, and if it had been tuned in any other way, life wouldn't have been as anyone would know it!

We looked at some evidence concerning the necessary conditions of life being supplied by our environment on

Earth, but this is just the tip of the iceberg. Carter and other scientists had plenty more up their sleeves to back up these new findings. Unfortunately they mean little to us non-boffins, but I will list a few of them anyway. All the following items are just right for making life possible, and if any one were even slightly different, life as we know it would be impossible: the rate of spin of the Earth, the length of a year, the tilt of the Earth, the diameter of the Earth, the strength of gravitation, the energy state of electrons and the power of the weak nuclear force. The list will be discussed later, with other factors added to it as the story develops.

So if any of these items weren't as they are, I wouldn't be writing this and you wouldn't be reading it. Sir Fred Hoyle, a world-renowned astronomer, stated: 'Common-sense interpretation of the facts is that a super-intellect has monkeyed with physics, as well as with chemistry and biology, and that there are no blind forces in nature.'[2]

As any GCSE Physics student will tell you, there are some naturally occurring numbers that are unchanging in the universe. They are called constants, because they are . . . constant, or unchanging. An example of this is *pi*, in geometry, a value used in calculating the area of circles. A very peculiar thing about these constants is that they appear to have exactly the right values. If they were slightly smaller or bigger, atoms, stars and people simply wouldn't exist. For instance, if the strong force inside atomic nuclei were just slightly stronger, it would boost the burning of stars so much that they would explode only seconds after they were formed. We wouldn't have a sun – or even a planet. If it were just slightly weaker, it would be too weak to hold together the stuff inside stars, including our sun, which just wouldn't light up any more.

Incredibly, the same goes for all other constants. As the Astronomer Royal, Martin Rees, puts it, 'The universe is "fine-tuned" by just six numbers, without which we would not exist.'[3]

Putting it in simpler terms, imagine you are in the universe Control Room, alone among the nothingness, at some time in the far-off past before anything existed. You are standing before a control panel with fourteen dials, each representing one of the forces, measurements or constants mentioned above and each calibrated with a hundred divisions. You are watching as, when each second ticks away, one dial moves to the next position, so that every possible combination appears just once. How long would you have to wait until every combination had been tried? Around a billion billion years by my reckoning. The reason why it's worth waiting is that just one combination of these dials produces a situation where intelligent life could spring up here on Earth. That's how improbable life is, particularly if we leave those dials to spin at random or according to a simple pattern.

Out of these ideas came something called the Intelligent Design movement, which recognized that because of the Anthropic Principle and because of observations of nature, there had to be a designer of all that we see around us and, since it all seems to be a pretty good design, this designer had to be intelligent. This was another controversial idea, as instead of bringing the scientific world and the religious world into harmony, there has been conflict over whether this is a scientific or a religious movement!

But the scientific community is nothing if not disunited, so not all are going to go along with this. Some scientists over the past few decades have been attempting to describe the origins of the universe with the aim of squeezing out the idea of any kind of intelligent designer. For them, Earth and humankind are not important, just an accident, a random event. For them, it all started at the Big Bang, a 'quantum singularity' or 'an expanding bubble of quantum foam appearing from nothingness' or, putting it simply, lots of very hot matter expanding very fast from one point. When asked who actually lit the blue touch paper of this Big Bang, most of them are not so sure of themselves.

There is an irony in this, as before the historical period known as the Enlightenment, scientists were theologians too and science itself was known as natural philosophy. A good example was Isaac Newton, who, when he wasn't making awesome discoveries in the fields of physics, astronomy and mathematics, was writing reams of theological material. In fact he wrote over four million words on theology and was said to be one of the greatest lay theologians of his age. Even John Wesley, the founder of Methodism and one of the greatest Christian evangelists of all time, also wrote books on medicine and electricity.

But times have moved on and the two worlds, by and large, have drifted apart, with apparently irreconcilable differences. Some, with a foot in each camp, try to bridge the gap, but are usually met with ridicule from the scientific establishment. The key issue is the one of Intelligent Design. To the modern scientific mind it is a throwback to an earlier, more primitive era, before science had begun to unlock the secrets of the universe, and they view this development with alarm and disdain.

So, Intelligent Design, eh? Where is all this leading? Without stating the obvious I will leave you with a familiar scenario. A kid receives his first train set for Christmas and, helped by Dad, pours out the contents of the box and proceeds to set it up. Their aim is to provide a fully operational train system whereby a scale model of a train chugs aimlessly round a circular track (I never did understand the appeal of such things). For this to happen we need a whole clutch of things to work together: the track all connected up correctly and seamlessly, a train correctly aligned on the tracks, an electrical supply to provide power, a system to convert this electricity into power for the wheels of the train and, of course, electricity itself and the funds to pay the electricity supplier. If any one of these things is absent you're left with one disappointed child! All are needed, working together in harmony.

In the same way, for life to be able to exist we need a whole swathe of things to be fitted together and to work together. The distance between us and the Sun and the Moon has to be just so. The forces that pervade the universe, from gravity to magnetism, have to be just so. The features of our Earth, such as its rate of spin and the composition of its atmosphere, must be just so. So many other things, too complex to describe, have to be just so.

If any of these are not just so, then so are we – we would never have been born because our planet wouldn't be here.

Where did our toy train set come from? Did it materialize out of nowhere or was it designed and put together by a toy manufacturer? If you accept the latter, perhaps we should be asking a similar question about Planet Earth.

Notes

[1] For more information on this conference and the Anthropic Principle in general, visit

http://en.wikipedia.org/wiki/Anthropic_principle

[2] Fred Hoyle, 'The Universe: Past and Present Reflections', pp. 8–12 in *Engineering and Science*, November 1981.

[3] Martin Rees, *Just Six Numbers* (London: Phoenix Press, 2000).

CHAPTER 2

THE END IS NIGH

It's a wonder you're still alive to be reading this, if you think about it. If the warnings presented to us with such earnest certainty by scientists, environmentalists, astronomers, astrologers, doom-merchants, Nostra-damn-us-alls and religious nuts had come true, we'd just be a collection of atoms spread over an area previously occupied by Planet Earth. Yet we've survived despite being told the following:

The millennium bug was going to mash up our digital world, at the least send us into a new technology-free dark age and at the worst scramble the brains of the military computers, thus unleashing a nuclear catastrophe. Or . . .

Armageddon was going to be unleashed by a vengeful, spiteful God, destroying the lot of us except for the Jehovah's Witnesses or Moonies or George W. Bush and selected friends. Or . . .

ET's relatives are not so cuddly and either have infiltrated us already, or make occasional forays with their anal probes, or are lurking above us in massive stealth spaceships. Either way they are apparently bent on world conquest, or perhaps they really are intending to build an intergalactic bypass. We wait with bated breath. Or . . .

Gamma-ray bursts from the cosmos are a phenomenon just waiting to happen. They've been everywhere else, zapping planets to smithereens. It's only a matter of time, apparently, according to some boffin pessimists. Or . . .

A new Ice Age has been predicted by some, ironically as a result of global warming. Apparently the melting of the polar ice caps would shut down the Gulf Stream, with consequences for humanity, not just the travel industry. Or . . .

The Kuiper Belt is apparently where the comets come from. Perhaps we're nearer than we care to be to the one of sufficient size and direction to do us a lot of damage. Or . . .

If the natural world doesn't get us, you can be assured that humanity will do its very best to self-destruct, with a vast array of options available. The bow and arrow and hand-to-hand fighting of old have been replaced by nuclear, chemical and bacteriological options for mass destruction. Or . . .

A mega-tsunami is a gigantic wave, big enough to cross oceans and destroy cities. They can be thousands of feet high, moving at supersonic speeds. The volcanic island of La Palma in the Canary Islands is the hot favourite to produce the big one that, at the very least, will completely destroy the east coast of the USA. Or . . .

Bird flu is the one they're all currently talking about: them pesky chickens in the Far East sneezing their germs into the human population. In terms of column inches this is the one that's really getting our scientists and politicians agitated. The outbreak of influenza in 1918–19 killed more people than the First World War and was said to be the most deadly epidemic ever. Perhaps the fears are justified this time?

Then there are the meteors, earthquakes, AIDS, SARS, plagues, nuclear, bacteriological and chemical disasters, volcanoes, and other scientific accidents producing artificial black holes, nanomachine infestations and quantum vacuum collapse. If one doesn't get you, there are plenty more possibilities waiting in line.

OK, some of these are plainly ridiculous and others have been shown to be flawed as new information comes to light. But it's a long list and growing longer, and surely they can't all be wrong. It only takes one of them to be right, after all.

Yet . . . none of them has been right, have they, because . . . we're still here, aren't we?

Why have they all been wrong so far? We all remember those scruffy individuals lurking with sandwich boards in shopping malls and high streets. 'The End is Nigh', they proclaimed. We still witness others with megaphones or just loud voices proclaiming a similar message, perhaps not with the same apocalyptic certainty, but a message of beginnings and endings nonetheless. But the end hasn't come, has it?

Why not?

A report accidentally published by US security chiefs on a website in Hawaii mentions fifteen doomsday scenarios dreamed up by a government department.[1] The list includes a nuclear bomb in a big city, plague released into an airport washroom and food laced with anthrax. The most costly would be a nuclear bomb driven in a van into a big city and exploded, causing hundreds of billions of dollars' worth of devastation. Much is made of biological and chemical attacks, with possibilities of terrorists spraying anthrax from aerosols as they drive from city to city. This is no report from the *National Enquirer* or *The Sun*; this came from government experts and so has credibility. It seems that governments, when they consider possible terrorist actions, are thinking in terms of when and not if. But a big 'when' hasn't arrived yet (well, not at the time of writing, anyway).

Why not?

The USA has five levels of readiness for war, from DEFCON 5, normal peacetime readiness, to DEFCON 1, 'If they just fart in our direction, we'll nuke the ***!!* out of them!' During the Cuban Missile Crisis, the US Strategic Air Command was placed on DEFCON 2 for the first time in history. On 6 October 1973, Egyptian and Syrian forces launched a surprise attack on Israel. On 25 October, US forces went on DEFCON 3 alert status, as possible intervention by the Soviet Union was feared.

These were close shaves, and in both cases they moved away from the brink when the danger was over and normality was restored. Although we may marvel and sigh in relief that the situation didn't reach a dreadful climax, we can understand why we were taken to the brink. After all, the Soviets had provoked both situations, and not to be ready for such an eventuality would have been seen as a great weakness, making war very likely.

But it hasn't always worked in expected ways. There have been false alarms that could have had horrendous consequences. Probably the best known false alert occurred in the mid-1950s, when a radar station mistook a flock of geese for a Soviet bomber attack. There have been at least four other less well known incidents in which the superpowers geared up for nuclear annihilation. All were caused by false alarms.

On 9 November 1979, at around 9 a.m., the computers at three major US military command centres all indicated the worst nightmare – a massive Soviet nuclear strike aimed at destroying the US command system and nuclear forces. Senior military officers and the missile defence system were primed for immediate response. The president's doomsday plane was even launched, but the president was not on board for a good reason – it was discovered that the whole episode had been generated by a training tape, accidentally inserted into the computer running the nation's early-warning programmes. Disaster was only averted because other defence systems were adamant there were no such missiles and someone peered out of the window and had a good look at the skies!

On 3 June 1980, another warning came through that the Soviet Union had launched a nuclear strike. Missiles were primed to retaliate and bomber crews were scrambled. This time, however, the computer displays didn't produce a consistent picture. In fact the whole system went haywire, with a random number of missiles being displayed, the number changing constantly. It turned out that a computer chip had gone bad and was responsible for the whole episode. Not so intel – igent, then? (Excuse the pun, if indeed you noticed it.)

It wasn't only the Americans who got it wrong; the Russians could also admit to the odd cock-up. On 26 September 1983, the Soviet early-warning satellite system caused a nuclear false alarm. They used a different method to the USA's to detect whether hostile missiles were on their way. Their satellites monitored just the edge of the Earth, rather than the whole planet, thus reducing the chance of mistaking naturally occurring phenomena for missile launches. On that fateful day, a trick of the light managed to fool this foolproof system and the Soviets really thought they were under attack. A nuclear war was averted thanks to the intelligence of the officer on duty, who reasoned that if the Americans wanted to start a nuclear war, they would do it with far more missiles than their readings indicated.

On 25 January 1995, Norwegian and American scientists launched a rather large rocket to collect scientific data. To Russian technicians, the flight path appeared similar to one that a US missile would take to blind their radar system by detonating a nuclear warhead high in the atmosphere. President Boris Yeltsin was poised to press the button for nuclear holocaust, but held back when new intelligence filtered through.

Now these are just the ones we know about, the ones that have been officially sanctioned for public consumption. But what about the others that we don't know about? Surely there are plenty more near misses that are simply too embarrassing or frightening to leak out. In fact, a comprehensive study of nuclear accidents has shown convincing historical evidence that despite measures taken to prevent them, such accidents are inevitable. But the inevitable hasn't come yet, has it?

Why not?

To put all this in perspective, there are about thirty-one thousand nuclear warheads in the world, of which around four thousand six hundred are ready for immediate use at a moment's notice. Just these latter missiles represent the firepower of 200,000 Hiroshima bombs. It's no joke. It only takes one random accident of nature, one human mistake. It's just as well that in the examples above fail-safes were in place to put things right. On the other hand, what happens when there are bad intentions?

In earlier days it mattered not a jot whether there were rogue nations bent on world domination, or demented dictators driven by twisted philosophies to destroy others who didn't fit within acceptable patterns. Unless they were stopped in their tracks by stronger opposition, the scope of their influence was limited by the distance a horse can gallop, or by the strain a lifetime of battle can put on a human heart, or by natural barriers, such as oceans or mountains. Genghis Khan and Alexander the Great may have conquered the world, but only that part of it known to them at the time, which wasn't that much of it really. Even Hitler and his allies, who got further than most, found the combination of Russian Bear, British Bulldog and American Eagle just a little too much. Even if he had conquered the world, his forces and those of his allies would have been spread too thinly to maintain a hold on the vast populations that would have come under his control.

But the world has changed immeasurably. Messianic ambitions are now matched by technological advances. Humanity can now actually destroy itself and there's a whole armoury of ways to do it, thanks to scientific endeavours in the fields of chemical, bacteriological and nuclear warfare. This was brought home by 9/11, the first event since 1066 known in this country just by its date. It showed that a determined group of individuals, motivated by a militaristic faith and funded by a rich, disaffected Saudi, were able to strike at the heart of the world's richest nation and set in motion a chain of events that led us into a new age of paranoia and uncertainty. Nowadays it's not just nations that can bring an end to it all. Technology of mass destruction is just a mouse-click away, and if a religious fanatic doesn't push the doomsday button, there's always the mad (or clumsy) scientist in a germ warfare lab who can unleash a new concoction of death into the world. But it hasn't happened yet, has it?

Why not?

Four times I have considered the possibility or probability of the world coming to a premature end and each time I wondered why it hasn't happened. Surely, just by looking at statistics, at probability theory, the odds must be so stacked against us that we've been living on borrowed time. Commentators have been telling us ever since 9/11 that a major terrorist campaign against Western nations on a similar scale has been imminent, yet it ain't come yet (at the time of writing, anyway). I find it hard to believe that it's been because of the skills and expertise of our military intelligence. Even the Israelis, famed for their intelligence network, have allowed occasional suicide bombers through to wreak devastation.

It only takes one major terrorist outrage, with weapons of mass destruction that have never been easier to get hold of, to change the world in ways that would make 9/11 seem like a nasty cough at a vicar's tea party. We hear of the near misses, of the 'An off-duty policeman noticed a strange bulge in the coat of a nervous-looking gentleman lurking outside Paddington station and immediately recognized him from a mug shot broadcast to his division earlier' variety and we wonder if this is just PR spin to placate us, to show us what a good job the authorities are doing, or to show us the need for heightened security even at the expense of personal liberty. Has a major threat just been averted, or are we being fed a line? One suspects the latter, but if the former is the case then we marvel at the fact that the world as we know it hasn't been disrupted and we can continue living our lives fairly normally.

But there's no doubt we have entered a new era of uncertainty. The world is no longer a safe place for those who up to now have lived their whole lives cosseted and secure in the knowledge that all the nasty stuff only happens on foreign fields. The terrorists have arrived over here and, whatever the rhetoric from our political leaders, fear has become a part of our lives. For many this fear can be overwhelming and can stifle thoughts of hope for the future. How can I bring children into such a world? Why plan for the future? Eat, drink and be merry, for tomorrow we die!

When the first bomb exploded in the London Underground on 7 July 2005, I was just a few trains behind. Afterwards I realized that 'there but for the grace of God went I', in that it could very well have been me if the terrorists had targeted Stratford station, in many ways an obvious target considering the 2012 Olympics decision made a day earlier. Casualties were low, because the bus bomb exploded outside the British Medical Association building and the London Hospital was hosting a convention for doctors at that time. Medical staff were aplenty, so the situation could have been far worse. Although not quite racked by survivor's guilt, I did wonder, when I saw the list of victims drawn from a multicultural mix of the nations, about the randomness of it all.

But life is like that. Consider the folk who argued with the driver of the number 30 bus, demanding to be let onto the overcrowded vehicle. He stubbornly refused and drove off, indifferent to their scowls. Minutes later that bus was gutted by the bomb, and how those folk must have counted their blessings and praised the actions of that driver. There can be many such episodes in our life, those 'what if' moments, when our life is presented with various possibilities and we spend the rest of it blessing or cursing the path that we took at that time. We can marvel that we are living in a country where food is plentiful, and with a welfare state to look after us when it is not. We are not at war with our neighbours, with real risks of death, torture, rape and pillage. We can consider ourselves lucky that we are where we are. Some call it Providence. Others thank Fate or Dame Fortune or Lady Luck, not realizing that they are invoking mysterious forces and minor deities.

Of course there is a flip side. There are unexpected bereavements, sudden illnesses and misfortunes that afflict us all to various degrees. Some people consider themselves blessed, others believe themselves cursed. All these scenarios suggest possibilities of something 'other' on the outside looking in. Is this just claptrap, or is there really someone or something watching over us?

The first terrorist outrage on British soil in many years could have been far worse. Conventional explosives had been used. The effects of chemical or bacteriological agents in the Underground system would have been horrendous. So far (at the time of writing) it hasn't happened, and I still ask the question:

Why not?

One possibility occurs, and it develops a theme introduced in the previous chapter. I suggested the possibility that our lives are part of some grand design, with a designer (or designers) who has put us on an Earth uniquely designed to support us. If that is so, perhaps this intelligent designer doesn't want us to screw it all up, doesn't want us to blow ourselves up before we have fulfilled our potential.

Perhaps we will screw it all up one day, but if we do, I'd rather that it made sense in the grand scheme of things, not that it all ended through an apocalyptic plague created by accident by a clumsy scientist in a research lab or at the whim of a crazed terrorist with the greatest suicide death wish of all!

Notes

[1] As reported the following day (17 March 2005) by *The Times* at http://www.timesonline.co.uk/article/0,,11069-1528458,00.html

CHAPTER 3

LIFE, JUST AS WE KNOW IT

There are plenty of things in this life that we accept as true. Sometimes we grow out of them as we grow up, as in the case of Father Christmas, the tooth fairy and a decent postal service. As we become more aware of the world around us, some previously accepted truths are discarded. Yet some are not, and we go through life believing the same old stuff mainly because nothing else has come along to teach us otherwise. This is fine as long as there's some semblance of truth in what we're believing. But there are some things that we may have been taught that were either untrue because our developing brains weren't ready yet (e.g. the birds and the bees as an explanation of 'you know what') or untrue because the world has moved on and better explanations have been put forward. This can be more important than you think.

Does the term 'primal soup' stir any brain cells? It was an experiment by Stanley Miller in the 1950s that claimed to produce life out of a 'soup' of chemicals placed into a container full of gases and energized with a swift bolt of electricity. The idea was that this combination reproduced the conditions all those millions of

21

years ago on Earth when life first appeared, and the experiment attempted to do the same thing in a laboratory. Remember it now? Still believe that it's the best explanation of how life came to be? Think again.

For the last twenty or thirty years this experiment has been totally discredited by the scientific community, yet that little gem of information hasn't filtered through to us, or to our education system. Objections include the fact that they made wrong assumptions about the gases and the amount of electricity that would have been needed to make it work. In other words, they managed to get most of the experiment wrong. Doesn't fill us with much confidence, does it? Yet some school textbooks still feature the experiment and, although others may add a warning that it's not the best fit for the data, it is included because the scientists haven't found a better fit, and they had to provide *some* explanation that reflected their world-view.

But deeper questions have been raised about the theory that life on Earth could have started in such a way.

'Life is just one damned thing after another,' said the writer Elbert Hubbard.

It is, too, you know. If you only realized how many 'damned things' need to be just right for the simplest life form to flicker into existence, your mind would truly be boggled. It's far more complicated than people ever realized. A million miles away from the myths and legends of old, the actual mechanisms of life processes have only recently been discovered, as a result of the new technologies now available and the disciplines that have come about, hanging on their coat-tails. There was a time when people thought that insect life was created when food went off, simply because that's where you would find these undiscerning eaters. If milk is left for a few days it goes cloudy with new microscopic life, but it doesn't mean that this life is created out of nothing. Again, these tiny organisms are just attracted by the food. Life is far more complicated than that.

Questions such as 'Where did we come from?' are answered these days by scientists following principles first proposed in the mid-nineteenth century by Charles Darwin under the all-encompassing umbrella of the Theory of Evolution. It has held sway ever since, with a firm grip on the hearts and minds of scientists the world over. Is that because it was a good theory? Not exactly. The problem is that it has been the only theory that science has come up with and, for many scientists, it has to be the only game in town because the alternative is unthinkable. We'll return to this alternative later.

Make no mistake, despite its billing as the enemy of organized religion, for most scientists working today in a whole variety of disciplines, the Theory of Evolution has become a religious system of the highest order. With a set of dogmas firmly entrenched in the past, based around the holy book *The Origin of the Species*, evolution is put forward as a mechanism to explain all the mysteries of life. It even has its priests, self-proclaimed spokesmen such as the biologist Richard Dawkins, to organize its worship. Dawkins has said, 'It is absolutely safe to say that if you meet somebody who claims not to believe in evolution, that person is ignorant, stupid, or insane (or wicked, but I'd rather not consider that).'[1] If that is not blind faith, I don't know what is! What it does remind you of, though, is the medieval church, zealous to protect its dogmas by vilifying the slightest deviation from them and burning 'heretics' at the stake.

So what's the attraction of the Theory of Evolution and how has it managed to attract such zeal?

A basic assumption of evolution is that life appeared by blind chance. The usual process, as already described, is that given a few million or billion years, a hotchpotch of chemicals swirling away in the right atmosphere will eventually produce the simplest form of life. From these will evolve, given a few more millions of years, simple organisms, which will, after a few more million years, modify and change with succeeding generations into more complex organisms, eventually producing human beings.

It's the process whereby the 'primal soup', given enough time, would eventually produce little old you and me, by way of amoeba, fish, small mammals and a variety of monkeys. It has reigned supreme in the scientific and educational community. The Natural History Museum is a virtual shrine to these ideas and school kids are spoon-fed on evolution as *the* explanation of the origins of life and humankind. Yet it is only a theory, and any scientist will tell you that a theory is just the best fit of available facts to explain a set of phenomena.

Many theories proposed by scientists of old have been replaced when new data has come to light that can't be explained by them. The baton is passed to a new theory that provides a better explanation for these new facts. For example, there was a time when ordinary folk believed that the Earth was flat. They believed it from observation and an incorrect reading of the Bible. Then along came the brave explorers, who sailed east and west and refused to drop over the horizon into the deep dark abyss, and the astronomer Copernicus, who provided the theory that the Earth was a globe, circling the Sun. So the old theory was disproved and abandoned by all save a few confused souls. That's the function of a theory: it's only there until something better comes along. Let's follow the lead of others, in an earlier time, who were faced with this very situation.

These people were scientists, naturalists, botanists, biologists. They were faced with a new way of looking at the world, a revolutionary new concept that went against all current wisdom and dogma. This new way of looking at the world was seductive to most, appealed to the intellect, and came with a set of 'proofs' that seemed to be conclusive. The only problem was that if you followed these new ideas, you would have to question all that was held dear and precious by the majority of your fellow countrymen. These were dangerous new ideas, but in time the scientific community was converted. Today, these ideas are considered the normal way of looking at the world.

Such is the history of the Theory of Evolution. When Charles Darwin first presented it to the scientific world in 1859, many saw it as an attack on the Bible and Christianity, which was the dominant world-view of that day. Until that time, the world had been considered created by God a few thousand years earlier. The Theory of Evolution stood that on its head, insisting that life had developed slowly over millions of years, from the simple cells in primeval ponds to the sophisticated thinking machines that make up the human race. Darwin was so nervous about the effects of his theory that he kept putting off the publication of his findings and turned himself into a physical wreck. He knew that he was going to upset the status quo, and particularly people who held to the old belief in a world created and sustained by God. To many people this new theory implied that the world was created and sustained by blind chance and not by God. It was a quantum leap: no wonder Darwin was a wreck. He had to be sure that his evidence and proofs were sustainable in order to convince scientists that he was presenting something authentic and believable. Let's look at them.

First, there were the fossils. What were they? They seemed to be remains of creatures from an earlier time and, on further analysis, some of these creatures seemed to have undergone changes when compared with their modern descendants. Surely these creatures had evolved? Then there were vestigial organs, parts of our body and the bodies of animals that seem to have no use but appear to indicate that they were 'left over' from a previous evolutionary state. Examples of these are the appendix in the human body and poorly developed limbs in some snakes. Then there was the similarity across species of various limb functions, such as the hand of humans, the leg of the horse and the paddle of the porpoise, seeming to indicate that all creatures have descended from common ancestors and that the limbs have evolved according to different needs. Another 'proof' was the observation that the foetus in the woman's body seemed to follow a transition that mirrored the accepted evolutionary wisdom of how a human being evolved from simpler species – from amoeba to fish, to small mammal, to ape, to human.

These evidences, along with other discoveries such as the weird and wonderful species found by Darwin on his journeys, were sufficient for many scientists to accept the Theory of Evolution as an explanation of how life began and developed. That's as may be, but we must not forget that evolution was never more than a *theory*, and when a theory is no longer supported by facts, it stops being a theory and starts being just another discredited bad idea. Why would I say this? Well, let's go back to the 'proofs' of evolution and see if they have stood the test of time.

Fossil remains did seem to offer a record of changes within species but, despite frantic searching over the last century and a half, vital 'missing links' that bridged species such as humankind and whatever came before us have failed to emerge. Darwin knew what a clincher this was. As he wrote, 'Why is every geological formation and every stratum not full of such intermediate links? Geology assuredly does not reveal any such finely graduated organic chain; and this is the most obvious and serious objection which can be urged against the theory.'[2] If found, these would have provided major evidence of evolution, particularly with regard to the origins of human beings. But they ain't been found yet!

Some of you might say, what about the archaeopteryx, the great dinosaur with wings? Weren't we taught that this was the 'missing link' between dinosaurs and birds? Since that 'discovery', scientists have explained that it was simply a strange-looking bird.

The vestigial organ argument, that other great pillar of the theory, has also been discredited. The crux of the argument is this: how is it that there are useless organs, such as the appendix, with no discernable function for our bodies? The conclusion is that these organs were useful for our 'evolutionary' ancestors and are still around in our body, just getting in the way. This was a mistaken belief: the appendix does have a function in the body. Its greatest importance is to the immune system, first to the developing embryo; later, it works to expose circulating immune cells to antigens from the bacteria and other organisms living in your gut. Similar stories can be told about other 'vestigial' organs in the human body and in the animal kingdom.

The 'evidence' provided by the development of the human embryo has also been discredited by scientists. Originally pointed out by Ernst Haeckel in the nineteenth century, it got Darwin all excited when he spoke of 'gill slits' appearing on human embryos at a certain stage of their development, indicating that we must have evolved from fish. The only problem is that this has been exposed as an out-and-out fraud and that Haeckel messed around with his results. Embryologists – who understand such matters – have occasionally pointed this out, but their findings have fallen mostly on deaf ears. In 1976, biologist William Ballard complained that so much energy continues to be 'diverted into the essentially fruitless 19th century activity of bending the facts of nature to support second-rate generalities'.[3] Yet some school textbooks still offer this as 'evidence' of evolution.

Next, the tree of life. You have heard of this. The Theory of Evolution states that the whole of life is descended from a single common ancestor billions of years ago, and this process can be viewed as a massive tree with endlessly dividing branches extending out from a trunk formed from the original simple life forms. Yet the evidence speaks differently. Most animal life forms appear suddenly, without ancestors, in what is called the Cambrian explosion about five thousand million years ago, according to dating methods favoured by evolutionists. It all happened so quickly: much too quickly for the usual evolutionary mechanisms. The tree of life just does not compute for these organisms.

Of course there is no time here to provide a solid, comprehensively reasoned rebuttal of the Theory of Evolution. All I can do is provide rough sketches of the problems that have emerged over the last century through further scientific discovery. The point I wish to make is that if the Theory of Evolution had been judged like any other scientific theory, it would have fallen apart by now, its credibility shot through because of its shaky foundations. But it has stood firm. Why?

To answer this question, we must remind ourselves of the dilemma of Charles Darwin just before he unleashed his bombshell of a theory on the world. He was very wary of the consequences of his findings, which went against the grain of the prevailing Christian world-view of nineteenth-century society. Scientists today are faced with exactly the same problem, but in reverse.

In Darwin's day there was a conflict brewing concerning the origins of the Earth and of life on it. Traditional views were of a God who created the lot, but it was also the Age of Reason and many scientists were reluctant to accept such an 'unscientific' concept. It was a time of great change; the Industrial Revolution was in full swing and science was held up as the source of answers to many questions that were being asked. For some scientists who had lost their belief in God, a new theory that seemed to explain many of the mysteries without the need for a supernatural being was a most acceptable development. If you believed in the Theory of Evolution, you didn't need to believe (or pretend to believe) in God any more.

Times have changed and the 'Age of Reason' has developed to such a degree that for the majority of the scientific and educational establishment, belief in God is seen as just a load of nonsense. Now that many of the 'evidences' for the Theory of Evolution have been discredited and many scientists are beginning to consider the possibility of Intelligent Design, we can see a mirror of the nineteenth century.

Today, the Theory of Evolution is *the* scientific world-view, the status quo in our classrooms, research labs, libraries and colleges. But the emperor has no clothes, or at least they are full of holes, and the one abiding reason for this is a great fear. It's a fear that 'perhaps much of what I base my life's work on is a false foundation'. It's also a fear of peer pressure, of anticipated scorn, rejection and loss of livelihood. But the fear goes deeper than that and can be explained when we consider the 'halfway house' proposed by many who have openly doubted the truths of evolution.

In July 2005, more than four hundred scientists put their name to the following statement: 'We are skeptical of claims for the ability of random mutation and natural selection to account for the complexity of life. Careful examination of the evidence for Darwinian theory should be encouraged.'[4] They have voluntarily 'outed' themselves, they have come out of the closet, willing to declare openly what their consciences and scientific integrity have told them is true. One man, Professor Anthony Flew, has gone further. A firm disciple of Charles Darwin for fifty years, he has done an about-turn in his later life. Science 'has shown, by the almost unbelievable complexity of the arrangements which are needed to produce life, that intelligence must have been involved,' he says. 'The argument for Intelligent Design is enormously stronger than it was when I first met it . . . it now seems to me that the findings of more than fifty years of DNA research have provided materials for a new and enormously powerful argument to design.'[5]

The professor is sure that there is an intelligent designer, but is not going any further. He stops just short of pondering metaphysical issues, but that doesn't mean we should do the same. Because if Intelligent Design is a valid alternative to the Theory of Evolution, who on earth is this intelligent designer?

Notes

[1] Richard Dawkins admits that he first made this quote in a *New York Times* book review in 1989.

[2] Charles Darwin, *The Origin of Species by Means of Natural Selection*, 6th edition (New York: Macmillan Publishing Co., 1927), Chapter 10, 'On the imperfection of the geological record'.

[3] William Ballard, 'Problems of Gastrulation: Real and Verbal', *BioScience*, 26: 1976, p. 38.

[4] *A Scientific Dissent from Darwinism*, The Discovery Institute, www.discovery.org

[5] Anthony Flew quoted in the video *Has Science Discovered God?* (Institute for MetaScientific Research, 2005).

CHAPTER 4

IT'S ALL IN THE DESIGN

'Ashes to ashes, dust to dust' must top the poll of 'last words you'd want to hear prior to death', as the implication is that you'd be lying in your coffin pondering the dreadful mistake that had been made and contemplating a rather nasty end. These words are derived indirectly from the Bible, where we are told that we are formed from dust and that's how we'll return to the ground at the end of our lives. A curious statement, but, as it turns out, not an incorrect one when we discover that clay and earth contain every single element found in the human body – just rearranged.

So how did that clay and earth become the sophisticated and marvellous living machine called the human body? Did it truly happen over millions of years by the blind process of evolution that is taught to us in schools? Do we accept this received knowledge, first dreamed up a century and a half ago, or do we investigate further with open minds?

The human body is amazing. It's not just our intelligence and moral qualities that separate us from the animal kingdom, it's the most wonderful way we are constructed, too. We are the only biped, meaning we're the only ones who walk on two legs, a feat that actually depends on ten separate features, from our straight back and upright skull to our angled femur bones and arched feet. Our feet alone are an incredible engineering feat, consisting of three arches, with three points of contact with the ground. Throughout our body are systems, structures and mechanisms that continue to amaze scientists as they conduct studies and begin to realize what a finely tuned machine they are looking at.

Charles Darwin was also impressed, and he could see the challenge that was presented to his Theory of Evolution, particularly when he considered some of the more sophisticated features of the human body. He wrote in his *Origin of Species*, 'If it could be demonstrated that any complex organ existed which could not possibly have been formed by numerous, successive, slight modifications, my theory would absolutely break down.'[1]

Now consider the knee joint. It is the most complex joint in the human body. It consists of four complicated parts that work together in a complicated mechanism. They are the upper leg bone (femur), the main lower leg bone (tibia) and the two cruciate ligaments. All four parts need to be in place in full working order, otherwise the joint won't work. Without going into details, there are sixteen critical characteristics of the knee joint, each essential to its working. If just one of these were missing, the joint wouldn't work. As each of these characteristics is defined by around one thousand bits of information, it is clear that many thousands of bits of information need to be just right for this mechanism to work.

Now examine this in the context of Darwin's admission that his theory would break down if something existed that couldn't possibly have been formed by numerous slight modifications. Evolution dictates that changes occur, one at a time, to adapt the functionality of an organ in a positive way. So, if the knee joint evolved, it must have been a slight improvement of whatever came before it. The trouble is that the joint needs sixteen things to work *just right* in order for it to function, and whatever came before it would not be a knee joint: it would not be anything workable. And if that were so, how could something totally useless be an improvement on whatever came before it?! It just doesn't compute – and that's not just my knee-jerk reaction!

The fact is that there are only three types of joint found in the human body (the other two being the pivot joint and the ball and socket joint), and the knee joint is totally different in every aspect to the other two. There is no possibility of an intermediate stage between them, as evolutionists would hope for. The knee joint is known to mechanical engineers as a four-bar mechanism. It is used in steering systems in motorbikes, systems designed and developed by engineers from detailed blueprints. Can you see my implication here?

Before we move on, here are three vignettes concerning parts of our body that we take for granted. Each is a jewel of design that puts our human engineering efforts to shame.

A remarkable feature of the human body is the foot, a marvel of engineering. It consists of twenty-six separate bones of various sizes and shapes, bound together by ligaments and supported by a system of muscles, fibres and blood vessels. The whole structure is nothing less than a miniature suspension bridge.

Not to be outdone by its lower neighbour, the hand has been described as the most sophisticated tool in the body. Each hand has thirty-five muscles and is capable of fifty-eight distinct movements. Its operation has provided such wonder for scientists that the thumb alone was described by Isaac Newton as convincing proof of a designer with intelligence.

Now to the eye. This really troubled Darwin, who wrote, 'To suppose that the eye, with all its inimitable contrivances for adjusting the focus to different distances, for admitting different amounts of light, and for the correction of spherical and chromatic aberration, could have been formed by natural selection, seems, I freely confess, absurd in the highest degree.'[2] And he wrote this before science uncovered exactly how complicated the eye and its systems actually are. As for how an eye could evolve out of anything else, this really stretches our incredulity. Until the umpteen interdependent systems that make up our optical system had come into place, we would have been as blind as a bat: we would have died out as a species through bumping into trees and tripping into swamps!

The best equivalent to the system of the human eye is the digital camera connected to a high-performance computer. The eye features auto-focus with a 'film' that is over a million times more sensitive than a camera film. It has been estimated that 10 billion calculations occur every second in the retina of the eye before the image even gets to the brain, a feat way too complex even for the most powerful computer in the world.

In the 1930s the new science of molecular biology was born. It was concerned with the workings of the cell and started to make major inroads into the way we understood the human body. Instead of understanding our bodies in terms of what could be seen and measured, such as the brain or heart or digestive system, this new science enabled us to investigate how things really worked, in terms of the chemical reactions that take place at the most basic level. If the Theory of Evolution was truly governing everything in the natural world, it needed to line up with the findings of molecular biology. So did it?

Between 1984 and 1994, one of the most prestigious journals covering this field published about twenty thousand papers. Only 2 per cent of these, however, dealt with how this new science fitted in with the Theory of Evolution in terms of how our bodies actually worked and how the systems within our bodies developed from the lower life forms that preceded us. If 'all was all right in the State of Texas', these journals would be packed full of neat examples and vindications of evolutionary thought. But it wasn't so, and so the priests and scribes kept their mouths shut. Books on the subject are virtually non-existent. The major textbooks dealing with biochemistry are also strangely silent on anything to do with evolution. So why is there a problem?

Let's look at that simplest life form, a single cell. It's the basic building block of life and there are billions of them in the human body. But we're going to work our way up, so this will be our starting point. The cell is made up of a central nucleus surrounded by fluid containing various chemicals, all packaged up within a membrane wall. It's a bit more than that really. A human cell may be tiny but a lot of stuff is packed into such a small space. There's the place containing instructions on what to do, the place where energy is produced, the manufacturing facility, the distribution centre, the storage centre, the waste disposal unit and the chemical production centre. All are separated from each other by a thin membrane within the cell.

Within this cell, stuff is always happening, just as in a well-oiled factory. The cell is continually producing chemicals called proteins, moving them around or disposing of them. To make sure everything works efficiently, it has at its disposal intricate and complex machines, just like any other factory. These machines are built to the highest specification and I will describe just one of them.

It is called the bacterial flagellum. It is, to all intents and purposes, an outboard motor, which propels the bacterium around to wherever it wants to go. This tiny machine has been described as the 'most efficient machine in the universe' and has forty working parts, despite needing to be magnified 50,000 times before we can actually see what's going on. It is mostly made up of three systems, all working together in harmony. First there is the paddle, which does the swimming, then the rotor mechanism that controls the paddle, and finally the motor that converts energy into the power that runs the whole shebang.

Once we finish marvelling at the sheer genius of a tiny machine working away so efficiently as it cruises around the stormy seas within the cell, we must pose one important question. Where on earth did a finely tuned machine with forty working parts come from? The Theory of Evolution tells us that this has developed from a simpler structure, which in turn developed from a simpler structure, and so on, and that this process took a rather long time. The problem is that the bacterial flagellum will only work if all forty components are in place. If just one component is missing, nothing works and there is no bacterial flagellum. Evolution just cannot cope with such a scenario, as it doesn't provide us with a situation in which *all forty* components are fully formed and operational as a cellular outboard motor.

It prompts us to ask the question, 'If it didn't evolve, where did it come from?' This question was posed in a different scenario in Chapter 1, and we were introduced to a concept that is becoming more popular among scientists – Intelligent Design. This argues that complex biological structures cannot arise by the random processes of evolution, but instead require a guiding intelligence. The issue is whether scientists are willing to admit the possibility that even their most cherished views might be wrong. Scientists have been wrong in the past and will continue to be wrong. The Theory of Evolution is one scientific theory that attempts to account for the history of life, but it's not the only kid on the block.

When we consider the bacterial flagellum, or any other of the marvellous machines and mechanisms within the human body, our minds can only fill with wonder as we try to imagine where they come from. Beyond the question of whether they have evolved by chance, or whether a designer is involved, there's a more important issue to consider. In our world, no machine or mechanism has simply appeared from nowhere. A watch or a car or a personal computer doesn't just assemble itself out of parts: there's always a blueprint to work from. Someone planned to manufacture it and set out a series of plans to show others how to do so. So what about our bacterial flagellum? Where did the plans come from, or does a cellular outboard motor just appear by accident?

This brings us to a wonderful, but complex, chemical known as DNA to you and me, or deoxyribonucleic acid to the initiated. DNA is where we find the blueprint for life, instructions for every process carried out within the human body. Incredibly, a single strand of it, stored within the nucleus of every cell in the body, is over two metres long when unravelled. It's no wonder it's so long if you consider that this chemical contains hundreds of millions of pieces of information that define every unique characteristic of the person.

What a clever chemical this must be, able to control the workings of our bodies, to say nothing of governing the continuation of life. In fact it's only clever in the sense that a computer is clever. A computer is only as clever as the person who designed it and the person who programmes it, providing the information, in the form of software, which does all the clever stuff. So what about DNA?

If you are a member of any generation prior to Generation X you will remember Morse Code. In the early nineteenth century, Samuel Morse devised a simple system for speeding up communications over large distances. It was a telegraph system and it depended on a code he developed, in which each letter was represented by a sequence of short signal bursts (dots) and long signal bursts (dashes). For example, the international distress signal SOS was transmitted as dot-dot-dot, dash-dash-dash, dot-dot-dot.

DNA works on the same principle. Instead of two 'bases' (dots and dashes) it has four bases, chemicals known as A, G, C and T (shorthand for adenine, guanine, cytosine and thymine). With Morse Code, information is sent as a series of dots and dashes, which will be meaningful to the receivers as long as they understand the code. With DNA, information is stored through a combination of the four bases, this information being vital for the development and function of all aspects of the human body.

How does DNA get there in the first place? It all starts at the point of conception. The human egg fertilized by the sperm already has enough information in it, thanks to the DNA, to fill tens of thousands of books. With this information, the new life created has all it needs to thrive in terms of every aspect of its workings and appearance. How DNA does this would fill a whole book and would boggle the untrained brain.

So the DNA in your body arrives there from your parents at the point of conception. In turn, their DNA comes from *their* parents, who received their DNA from their parents. And so it goes on, back through the generations, until . . .

Well, it all depends on your viewpoint, because what is happening is that just as Morse Code transfers information through dots and dashes, so DNA transfers its information through the four bases. But there is a difference, because the information encrypted into Morse Code comes from a human being, the person who creates the message. In the case of DNA we really have to decide where the information first comes from. Do we trace it back millions of years to the 'primeval swamp'? In that case you still have to ask how the first DNA molecule came to be. Where did the information come from then, or was it a random combination of the four bases that just happened to have sufficient information to kick-start life? Alternatively, we can consider what seems to be patently obvious – the information in the DNA had to be provided by some kind of intelligent being, our intelligent designer.

This is more or less implied by no less a luminary than Bill Gates, the founder of Microsoft. He has said, 'DNA is like a software program, only much more complex than anything we've ever devised.'[3] This is a telling statement. Is he suggesting that a chemical that evolved through blind chance is cleverer than some of the best software designers in the world, or is he conceding the possibility of design?

Science magazine, celebrating its 125th anniversary, published what it reckoned were the Top 25 big questions facing science today and in the near future. It is interesting to see that five of these questions take us right into the heart of our benign conspiracy and another five skirt its periphery. One of the questions posed was, 'How and where did life on Earth arise?' The writer Carl Zimmer concedes, 'Because DNA and proteins depend so intimately on each other for their survival, it's hard to imagine one of them having evolved first. But it's just as implausible for them to have emerged simultaneously out of a prebiotic soup.'[4]

DNA and the origins of life create a great perplexity in many scientists today. You will notice that in many school textbooks and educational websites today, there is a growing admission that the Theory of Evolution has no real answer to this, but they skirt the problem with an almighty fudge. For a clue, here is a letter to *The Times* (12 July 2005), written by the eminent scientist, Professor Chandra Wickramasinghe.

> Sir, the spectacular impact of a space probe onto a comet has made astronomical history . . . The question that concerns us above all else is whether comets could have been connected with life on Earth. The idea that they may have seeded our planet with the chemical building blocks of life, or even perhaps fully fledged primitive life, was discussed by the late Sir Fred Hoyle and myself in the late 1970s . . .

This view seems to be quite widespread among evolutionists. What it is saying is, 'We haven't a clue where life came from, so let's give in to the science fiction writers and concede that "it came from outer space".' It means that they have no other credible theory and are willing to grab at any available straws.

Perhaps one day the scientists will figure it all out with an elegant solution firmly within the mindset of evolutionary thinking. But until then, they will continue to look outwards rather than inwards for their answers to the question of life's origins.

Notes

[1] Charles Darwin, *The Origin of Species by Means of Natural Selection*, 6th edition (New York: Macmillan Publishing Co., 1927), p. 179.

[2] ibid p. 167.

[3] Quoted by Stephen Mayer in *Discovery Institute News* (2 December 2005), www.discovery.org.

[4] http://www.sciencemag.org/sciext/125th/

CHAPTER 5

OUR DARKEST HOUR

It was Britain's darkest hour. The events over the period of a few months in 1940 would determine the future, not just of our own country but of the whole world. The Nazi menace was on our doorstep, peering in and already salivating over the expected spoils. The odds were on their side: they had proved invincible in Europe, each country falling in turn, like a cascade of dominoes. We were next. Defeat for us was unthinkable, no less than the destruction of a civilization that had stood unshakeably for nearly a millennium.

In the spring of 1940 the Nazi Third Reich was one of the largest empires the world had ever seen. It directly controlled or influenced almost all of continental Europe and large parts of North Africa, and had not been defeated. Adolf Hitler seemed invincible. German war casualties had been minimal and most of the people were totally behind their deranged Fuhrer. On 10 May he launched his forces against France and Belgium. It was over in two weeks and the British army found itself trapped and encircled, mocked by the Nazis' boast that they were moving in for the kill.

Our army, numbering over three hundred thousand, was stranded, and the only salvation was a full-scale evacuation across the English Channel. This withdrawal, at Dunkirk, has been well documented and has the unique distinction of being a day of both national setback and national heroism. On the BBC website it is described as the 'miracle' of Dunkirk and Churchill himself called it 'a miracle of deliverance'. So what made this so special?

Where shall we start? First, the manner of the rescue. These soldiers weren't just rescued by a convoy of warships and merchant vessels, but also by a hotchpotch of craft – yachts, fishing boats, rowing boats, motor boats, some taken there by their owners, eager to 'do their bit'. It was a truly heroic civilian operation. Secondly, there was Hitler's curious decision to hold his troops back and not attack the trapped British army. This was later described by some historians as Hitler's first really fatal mistake of the war. Thirdly, there was the matter of the German air force. It was stranded in Flanders, hemmed in by a furious storm and unable to attack the retreating boats. Fourthly, the fact that despite this storm a few miles away, the English Channel was still and calm. Finally, the fact that when some German planes did manage to attack, casualties were very low. A curious combination of factors that ensured that for those who witnessed Dunkirk, 'miracle' seemed to be the first word that came to their lips.

We move on a few months to the summer of that same year.

No one expected Britain to hold out; even the Americans contacted Churchill and asked if the Royal Navy would be sent to Canada when England fell. 'We will survive, not surrender!' growled Winston Churchill, our wartime leader. It was brave rhetoric, as few believed him in their heart.

The German air force – the Luftwaffe – was poised. If the Nazis were to mount a successful invasion, there was a small matter of the British air force, the RAF, to deal with first. It *was* a small matter: after all, Germany had almost two thousand eight hundred operational aircraft, against some nine hundred British fighters. There were also few pilots in Britain: many had already been lost and numbers had to be made up with untrained youngsters and an overseas contingent from the British colonies and other countries.

Hermann Goering, head of the Luftwaffe, had promised Hitler that his force could destroy the RAF prior to the seaborne assault on Britain, at which time some 260,000 German troops would be landed along the English coast.

It began on 13 August, with attacks on the British airfields and radar stations. The Battle of Britain had started. These attacks continued through to 24 August and the RAF suffered greatly. Almost 25 per cent of their pilots were lost, and if the Germans had continued these attacks, the RAF would surely have been destroyed. But Goering then changed tactics, switching the attack from the airfields to the control centres, which sustained major damage, severely compromising the command infrastructure.

The Luftwaffe was also losing many planes, but, as they had so many more than the British, they coped with this. Hitler was itching for the invasion, and good weather would not last past September. They had to act soon. The writing was on the wall.

Then something strange happened . . . A student of history comes across these instances quite often. Human affairs are sprinkled with little accidents, unforeseen factors, errors of judgement, illogical decisions and the like. Sometimes they are insignificant in terms of consequences, but occasionally they alter the course of major events.

There's a huge list of them: the Charge of the Light Brigade, Custer's last stand, Napoleon's Russian campaign, Hitler's Russian campaign, and all attempts at taming Afghanistan, to name but a few. Military and world leaders who overstep the mark sometimes manage to shoot themselves in the foot, through a combination of madness, pride and sheer bad luck.

So what *did* happen to derail Hitler's ambitions? A single German airman altered the course of history. Stuck in a fog over London and tired after a long day of mayhem, he mistakenly dropped the remainder of his bombs over the City of London on 24 August – a civilian rather than a military target. Winston was incensed and the RAF responded by mounting a major raid on Berlin the following night. Causing only minor damage, this raid embarrassed Goering, who had promised Hitler that Germany would never be bombed. An enraged Hitler ordered Goering to switch the bombing campaign to London civilian targets in retaliation.

On 7 September the Blitz began. German bombers appeared in force over London, and for the next fifty-seven nights they would pound Britain's cities in an attempt to break the will of the British to fight. Although a tragedy for the civilian population, it eased the pressure on the RAF, which was unexpectedly given time to replenish its supply of aircraft and trained pilots. The key day was 15 September.

In his war memoirs, Churchill cites this as 'the culminating date' in the Battle of Britain. He tells how he visited the RAF Operations Room that day and watched the progress of the battle in the skies, as the Luftwaffe attacked and attacked. At one point he asked the Air Marshal, 'What other reserves have we?' The answer came: 'There are none.' Then another five minutes passed, and he later wrote, 'It appeared that the enemy were going home. The shifting of the discs on the table showed a continuous eastward movement of German bombers and fighters. No new attack appeared. In another ten minutes the action was ended.'[1] The Luftwaffe had had enough and decided to go home, snatching defeat from the hands of victory.

It was, in fact, the end of the Battle of Britain, and soon afterwards Hitler ordered the indefinite postponement of his invasion plans.

So Hitler was thwarted in his plans for Britain. His plans were certainly achievable: historians are clear on this. But we're not all eating bratwurst at McGoebbels or attending compulsory Wagner recitals at the Royal Adolf Hall. So what went wrong (or right, depending on your perspective)?

When we review the facts of that momentous year we can identify two key moments, hinges of history, when the most significant events took place. The first was in late May, when the British army was evacuated at the 'miracle' of Dunkirk. The second was on 15 September (now known as Battle of Britain Day), at that crucial moment of the Battle of Britain when the Luftwaffe just gave up.

Believe it or not, there is one act that ties those two dates together, an unprecedented decision of the reigning royal, King George VI, to call the whole nation . . . to prayer. This he did two days before Dunkirk and seven days before Battle of Britain Day. Two days when the churches of Britain were packed to the rafters, with Westminster Abbey boasting the sort of queues that wouldn't embarrass a U2 concert. Now, Christianity was in decline in those days, many smarting over the carnage of the First World War and blaming God for the loss of a generation of young men in the trenches of Flanders. But a spark remained and these were trying times, so, on those two days in 1940, Christian Britain prayed as never before.

They prayed, and the deliverance at Dunkirk occurred. Then they prayed again, and the Battle of Britain was won. What can we say about this? We can accept that both cases were coincidences, that the outcome would have been the same if they hadn't prayed. We can never know; we don't live in multiple time lines like the hero of some sci-fi TV series. The calls to prayer were made at times of sheer desperation, at times when everything else had failed, all human resources were exhausted and the future was grim, grim, grim. Deliverance didn't seem possible at the time: just read Churchill's diaries for the evidence of this. Joseph Kennedy (the father of JFK), who was the US ambassador to Britain in 1940, was in no doubt that Britain would fall. In May he urged all Americans living in Britain to go home, as he did himself shortly afterwards. But deliverance came, despite the low expectations, and we have to ask whether the prayers had any effect on the outcome.

Without going into further detail about the mechanisms involved, we may be forced to concede that either the act of praying itself or the result of praying had unlocked unseen powers of deliverance. Did these acts really change history, or is this just a fanciful notion? We must have an open mind about such things and be thankful that if events really were changed, our country experienced something remarkable and special.

This was acknowledged after the war by Air Chief Marshal Lord Dowding, Commander-in-chief of Fighter Command in the Battle of Britain. He noted: 'Even during the battle one realised from day to day how much external support was coming in. At the end of the battle one had the sort of feeling that there had been some special Divine intervention to alter some sequence of events which would have otherwise occurred.'[2]

Back to our benign conspiracy: as we saw in Chapter 2, it seems that the affairs of humankind are not always in our own hands and there's often more to our daily existence than meets the eye.

These 'National Days of Prayer' are no more in our country: perhaps we don't discern the need for them. Churches (and no doubt synagogues and mosques too) were fuller than usual after the London bombings in July 2005, but that was down to individual choice rather than a national movement. These days only pop stars have the power to motivate us to action on a national scale. It's a funny old world, isn't it?

But these prayer days are not dead and buried. The baton has been firmly seized by the USA, which conducted one after 11 September 2001, at the instigation of President Bush. There are also moves in that country to make this an annual event.

Perhaps a day will come in the near future when our nation is in a similar position to the one in which it found itself back in 1940. Who will we call on then to save us, God or Bob Geldof?

Notes

[1] For a full account of this episode go to http://www.winstonchurchill.org/i4a/pages/index.cfm?pageid=671

[2] Quoted in *Rees Howells, Intercessor* (Cambridge: Lutterworth Press, 1952), by Norman Grubb, p. 262.

CHAPTER 6

THE EYE OF THE BEHOLDER

This chapter may be seen as a bit of an indulgence. It's the most subjective and personal, but no less important than the others. I will start with a list.

My list includes (in no particular order) an autumn sunset, the Barbarians' 1971 try against the All Blacks, my wife (more so, the older she gets), the Orion nebula and Pythagoras' theorem. My wife responds with her own: a toddler's giggle, Mt. Skiddaw from the south-west, a garden in full flower and a fruity white wine. We are talking beauty here, in case you haven't guessed yet. Some items could appear on others' lists, others are purely subjective: the eye of the beholder and all that.

Consider the clouds. Look beyond the water vapour, angry storms and sunlessness. Instead, lie on your back for five minutes in the garden and give free rein to your imagination. See the ever-shifting kaleidoscope of whites and greys, the interlocking levels, the merging, the fading, the sudden appearance of complexity. See Jimmy Durante becoming Charles de Gaulle. See the child-catcher disappearing into the hind quarters of an elephant. See it all for free and wonder. Or be unmoved and just see them as the harbingers of rain and obstructers of suntans.

How about taking yourself off to a secluded space and spending just five minutes listening, watching, smelling and feeling? I sat on a bench by a boating lake and was amazed by just how many sounds I was able to pick up: three different types of birdsong, the faint hum of traffic and farm machinery, the jarring quack of ducks, the gentle lapping of water, the barking of a dog, the distant chatter of schoolkids, the rumble of a plane overhead.

I asked myself, is this beauty? And if there was beauty in what I experienced, would it be beauty for you too? Is there an absolute beauty or is it really in the eye of the beholder?

Beauty is defined as that which gives pleasure to the mind or senses, and I'd be the first to admit that not all I experienced then would fit that definition. Take the birdsong, for instance. Apparently a bird's song typically lasts around four seconds and a chaffinch can sing up to forty-five notes a second. Some birds can sing two notes at the same time and the nightingale actually sings harmonies. Many birds are said to have perfect pitch and some can even change key in mid-song. So it's not just random warbling: there's a lot of talent out there in the bird world. I believe birdsong has beauty, because although the purpose of the singing is communication between birds, we humans can also derive pleasure from it for no practical reason save the sheer enjoyment of it.

Beauty can even be found where the natural world meets the human world. There are two days in the year when the Sun does something interesting in the Manhattan district of New York. It sets in a way that corresponds perfectly with the street grid. This means that it lines up perfectly with every street, so if you travel south and look to the west you'll be dazzled by the setting Sun at every junction. Someone remarked that it makes Manhattan a type of modern Stonehenge. Now I would find that beautiful, though I doubt if many busy New Yorkers would see it as anything other than a frustrating distraction.

Returning to the question of whether there is an absolute beauty, the answer must be yes, otherwise there wouldn't be such a thing as aesthetics, and art galleries would be a waste of time as no one would be able to decide what to exhibit. There are things of beauty that would be greeted with universal approval, as sales of celebrity magazines and fashion items prove. Streetwise maidens quite readily marry rich octogenarians because each finds beauty in the other, whether it's the beauty of youth or the beauty of a bursting bank account.

So what is beauty? Why David Beckham, Kate Beckinsale and the Porsche Carrera? Why not a bulldog, a pot-belled pig and the Citroen 2CV (just my opinion)? The majority of people living in our country would agree with this assessment. Why?

An answer can be found in the curious world of mathematics.

There is a special number. It's called *phi*, the Golden Section, the Golden Number, or the Divine Proportion. It's 1.6180339887. What a beautiful number, is it not? It is, but not in an obvious way. It is actually a geometric ratio of intersecting lines, which is probably all you need to know for now.

What's really strange and fascinating about this number is that it appears all over the place in mathematics, nature and the universe. It can be seen when we examine the human body, plants, the Solar System, art, architecture, music, even the Bible and the stock market. It's a persistent little critter!

In mathematics it is found in an interesting sequence called the Fibonacci series. This is reasonably easy to follow. It is a sequence of numbers formed by adding together the two preceding numbers. It's best demonstrated by looking at it:

0, 1, 1, 2, 3, 5, 8, 13 . . .

$0 + 1 = 1$
$1 + 1 = 2$
$1 + 2 = 3$

Fibonacci, the thirteenth-century mathematician, first saw this sequence acted out in nature when he studied breeding rabbits and discovered that the family tree, as it unravelled, followed our sequence of numbers. It can also be seen in nature in the creation of spiral structures, as in sea shells, and in the number of petals on a plant – a lily has three petals, a buttercup has five, delphiniums have eight, and so on. Staying in the botanic realm, it can also be seen in the arrangement of seeds on flower heads and of leaves around their stems, and in the structure of pine cones. It also features in the structure of the human ear!

To get to our Golden Number, *phi*, from the Fibonacci series, you simply add each number to the one after it and divide by this last number. Each new fraction produced inches closer and closer to *phi*. Try it and you'll see what I mean (or just take my word for it, whatever's good for you).

Phi has been used to create perfect acoustics in the design of music studios and cathedrals. Stradivarius used it in the design of his world famous violins, and it has also been used by the designers of all sorts of musical items, from saxophones to loudspeakers.

So *phi* appears all over the place. There's something about the proportions that it represents, whether in the appearance of pine cones or in a painting. To our human minds it produces a sense of balance and harmony, and we call this beauty. It's no surprise that something occurring in nature that is guaranteed to produce beauty should be used by our creative minds to produce art, architecture and music.

The Ancient Egyptians used *phi* in the creation of their pyramids, as did the Greeks in the design of the Parthenon and other buildings. Leonardo da Vinci knew all about it (no surprise there), and it was also used in the design of Notre Dame in Paris. A modern-day application of the Golden Number is in the construction of the United Nations building in New York.

Da Vinci used it in his art. All key dimensions in 'The Last Supper' were carefully calculated using *phi*, known at that time as the Divine Proportion. A more recent 'Last Supper', painted by Salvador Dali in the twentieth century, made heavy use of the Divine Proportion, even down to the positioning of the two disciples either side of the Christ figure. Georges Pierre Seurat, the French impressionist, was a great devotee of the Divine Proportion, using it in all his paintings.

Bringing the whole argument back to the subject matter of this chapter, we can apply *phi* to the human face (not literally, of course). Dr Stephen Marquardt has done so, and has used this mathematical model to create a plaster cast model – a beauty mask – of the most beautiful shape a human face can have. He believes that there is an 'ideal face' lurking deep in our consciousness, with which we compare everyone we meet. This hidden face is hidden no more, according to the good doctor, though rumours abound that his beauty mask was last seen in Beverly Hills, walking around on rich, ageing bodies.

So how was he able to use this ugly-looking number, 1.6180339887, to produce the ideal face? It's all about proportions, the distance between the eyes and the mouth and the nose and the chin and the ears. Even the positions of the teeth and the width of the smile are taken into consideration. It all boils down to geometry really, and every measurement made is bound up in this Golden Number. So the next time someone tells you you're ugly, get your tape measure out and prove them wrong!

There are other numbers that occur in the mathematical universe. One of them is 3.1415926535. Not as beautiful as 1.6180339887, but a lot more famous. This is *pi*, as in 'pi r squared', the area of a circle. Anyone with a general education would be familiar with *pi*, but few would know that our two numbers *pi* and *phi* are loosely related, and that if you multiply them together you enter the realm of 'golden geometries', and also into some very questionable mystical areas. Another number is c, the speed of light, as popularized by Einstein in his famous equation, $E=mc^2$. There are other significant numbers in the realms of physics, cosmology and other scientific disciplines, and to list them all here would simply bore us all to death.

What is incredible about these numbers is how they appear all over the place, as glue within the fabric of the formulae and equations that underpin the workings of the universe. If you think about it, there is real beauty in this. The whole universe, from the microscopic to the macroscopic, runs according to the laws of mathematics. It's truly mind-boggling and you really do need 'a brain the size of a planet' to understand it on all levels. We don't need to understand it, though, just to appreciate it and, perhaps, to ask one tiny question: why?

Well, they never told me at school that mathematics could be beautiful – but there's plenty they held back from me at the time by not telling me how cruel the world is, what with the rat-race, mortgages and the like. It's all a question of assuming an open, even childlike, attitude to the world around you and looking at things afresh, appreciating things that you've always taken for granted. It doesn't cost, so why not try it?

There is little evidence that animals appreciate beauty, so this seems to be a privilege offered to us human beings. It's not essential for life, it doesn't put food on the table (unless you're in the beauty business), it doesn't protect you from the elements and it doesn't protect you from your enemy. It doesn't have value in a material sense, but our lives are far richer as a result of it. Consider it as a free gift from whoever created it, or, of course, if you prefer, you could raise your glass to the millions of years of randomness that produced the dazzling sunset, the perfect symmetry of the snowflake or the majestic nuances in the song of a chaffinch.

CHAPTER 7

GHOSTS IN THE MACHINE

From where you are sitting, list all the gadgets around you that were unknown, say, fifty years ago. My list includes my trusty Dell PC, digital camera, mobile phone, iPod, fax/answering machine, satellite receiver and VCR. Can you imagine going back in time and telling your great-grandfather that in fifty years' time he would be able to speak and send pictures to people anywhere in the world from the top of a hill and record messages (and receive written replies) from them, listen to 20,000 pieces of music in full stereo through a tiny earphone, pick up hundreds of TV channels and record them for future viewing and, from a desktop box of tricks, explore a 3D universe, create and study writings, pictures, sound and moving images from thousands of miles away and run a small business. I can't even believe it now and I'm living in the middle of it!

We take technology for granted. It makes life easier; it entertains us and informs us. Never before has electricity opened up such exciting horizons. We are spoilt for choice, particularly in our leisure time activities.

As this is a book about secret conspiracies, it is fitting to look at the role of technology, as there is a perfect marriage between it and some of the more paranoid conspiracies of the Big Brother and New World Order variety. Technology has given us spy cameras, surveillance satellites, CCTV and huge intrusive databases that know your shoe size as well as your National Insurance number. It is grist to the mill for the suspicious anorak who sees the all-seeing eye of the state everywhere and who could have a point, as there are some areas in London that have the highest concentration of surveillance cameras anywhere in the world.

But all this is common knowledge, and I'd rather that we look at technology in a different way. In our gradually unfolding conspiracy, technology has not always been considered a friend, yet there is great potential for a marriage made in heaven – literally. It is the heavens that we will make our first port of call.

The telescope has come a long way since Galileo had his wrist slapped by the church for peering at the night sky and daring to believe that the Earth moved round the Sun. His telescope could magnify around eight times, which meant that the moons of Jupiter could be observed as tiny pinpricks. Four centuries later, our telescopes see them as huge rocky giants hurtling through space. Indistinct blobs and smears in the sky now become starry beacons of beautiful geometric complexity. As telescopes increase in power, more and more of the stellar landscape is unwrapped for us and we marvel at the beauty revealed therein.

Astronomers now have an array of technology at their beck and call, from radio astronomy to imaging technology and adaptive optics. And if all that breaks down, they've still got a backyard and a sturdy set of binoculars! They have all they need to make sense of it all, and so it is interesting for us to find out what conclusions they have come to, now that they have the technological firepower to prise the secrets out of our stubborn universe.

They have made a set of observations that has shaken the more deep-thinking of their number to the core. We are back to the Anthropic Principle, as introduced in Chapter 1, but here we are filling in the gaps and documenting the conclusions made. This can be a bit wordy but I will try to simplify as we go on.

First we look at those numbers, called constants, that are found when we observe the universe. They are the gravitational, electromagnetic, and strong and weak nuclear force constants. If these were even the slightest bit larger, there would be no small stars, no hydrogen, and no heavy elements. If they were slightly smaller, there would be no large stars, and no elements apart from hydrogen. In other words, the universe would have very little in it, and certainly none of the building blocks for life.

Then there is the ratio of protons to electrons in the atom. Any slight deviations here would mean a completely empty universe. Other setbacks would occur if there was any difference in the age of the universe, the spread of radiation, the distance between stars, the brightness of the Sun, the speed of light and a whole load of other factors that would mean even less to you than to me. The suggestion I wish to make is that rather than trying to understand the implication of these discoveries ourselves, we look instead at the effect they have had on eminent scientists, particularly at the point when it was all sinking in among the scientific establishment.

As mentioned earlier, the astronomer Fred Hoyle concluded in 1982 that 'a superintellect has monkeyed with physics, as well as with chemistry and biology.' In 1984 Paul Davies conceded that 'the laws [of physics] . . .

seem themselves to be the product of exceedingly ingenious design,'[1] and that there was for him 'powerful evidence that there is something going on behind it all. The impression of design is overwhelming.' In 1988 George Greenstein said, 'As we survey all the evidence, the thought insistently arises that some supernatural agency . . . must be involved.'[2]

The more deeply astronomers investigate the origin and development of the universe, the more evidence they accumulate for our benign conspiracy. And this evidence has been provided by technological advances in the world of science, an area always regarded as opposed to the world of the metaphysical and supernatural. Time and time again, honest scientists are realizing that the only explanation for the universe we observe is the action of an entity beyond the space-time continuum that is capable of design and of carrying out that design. It's that intelligent designer again!

Moving from the 'too big to imagine' to the 'too small to imagine', we now enter the microscopic world. Here we find a different story, because rather than dealing with the abstract world of physics, of weird and mysterious forces and constants, we can – electronically rather than optically – view the evidence for ourselves (assuming we have a few million quid to spend on an electron microscope).

We have already looked at the bacterial flagellum, that tiny miraculous outboard motor. It was given as an example of clever design, but it's not the only example: it's just the tip of the iceberg.

Consider the *cilia*, hairs on the surface of cells. One of their functions is to help you cough up phlegm, the uncouth little tykes! Another function is to propel sperm around: quite an important duty, I would say. They look like minute hairs until investigated closer with an electron microscope, which reveals that they are highly complex machines, made from two hundred parts. They achieve movement through a rowing motion, produced by a three-component mechanism. Each of these components is vital; the lack of any one would mean no movement is possible. So all parts have to be in place at the same time for the cilium to do its job. The possibility that all two hundred parts have each evolved through a separate path towards the production of this sophisticated and fully operational machine is frankly ridiculous, and it has never been satisfactorily explained by evolutionists.

Then there is the blood-clotting process. We take it for granted, but we'd soon notice if this complicated procedure failed to work – we would bleed to death! This is a ten-step process, using twenty tiny molecular machines. It has become something of an embarrassment to evolutionists. There's an obvious flaw in their thinking here: how can the mechanism of blood-clotting have developed over time, step by step? What's to stop the animal or person from bleeding to death in the meantime? You need the complete system in place before blood-clotting can actually occur; there's no avoiding the fact. As with the cilia, the blood-clotting system can realistically only be viewed as an off-the-shelf package from the heavily stocked supermarket owned by our intelligent designer and operated through the benign conspiracy franchise.

Of course, without technology none of these marvellous processes could be observed and examined, so the technical prowess of humanity is drawing us ever closer to the heart of the benign conspiracy.

There is one technological advance that has made the greatest impact on our society. It started life as Colossus, a monster machine created in 1941 by the boffins at Bletchley Park as a wartime code-breaker. It was a power-hungry giant, filling a large room and operating on the basis of 1,500 glass valves. It was also the world's first computer and had a significant role to play in defeating the Nazis, but that's another book!

We're a lot more blasé these days about our computers, calling them PCs and Macs and allowing them to run our home businesses and to meet our entertainment needs – and to run down our disposable income, with their (or our) constant need for add-ons, software and downloads.

Yet this soulless box of tricks has opened up an interesting and surprising area and has inadvertently provided us with a glimpse of the benign conspiracy. Computers have great processing power, meaning that they have the ability to crunch more numbers in a second than the average brain could cope with in a week of stretching and straining. In 1988 a small group of Jewish scholars put this to the test. The surprising subject of their number (or letter) crunching was that ancient, maligned book – the Bible. Following research by an earlier scholar who didn't have the technology, they believed that a computer could unlock secrets that had been hidden in that book for many centuries.

They picked three hundred pairs of words, such as man and woman or tree and leaf, and asked the computer to analyse the first book of the Bible to see if these words could be found within the text. Before you object, let me add that they were viewing the text as a continuous flow of letters, with no spaces between the words; otherwise it would have been a simple and pointless task. Another condition was that the letters of the words they were looking for would not necessarily be consecutive (i.e. next to each other) but at regular intervals. So, for instance, when the computer looked for the 'm' of the word 'man' (in Hebrew, of course), if the 'a' wasn't found next to the 'm' it would look for the 'a' at a two-letter interval from the 'm', then at a three-letter interval, until it found it. When it found it, it would then look for the 'n' at the same interval, and if it found that, it would register its findings. Now you can see why a computer was needed!

So what was that all about? The incredible thing was that every single one of those three hundred words was found, every one of them next to its pair. The astounding fact was that the chances of this happening naturally were infinitesimal, and the only conclusion they could draw as research scientists and mathematicians was that they were put there on purpose. By whom? The people who originally wrote down those Hebrew letters thousands of years ago? Remember, the text of this first book, the book of Genesis, was a historical account of the creation of the world and of humans, and the early history of the Jewish people. Even with a computer (which of course they didn't have), how on earth could the authors write this history and include, hidden in the text, these three hundred word-pairs?

Was there anything else hidden in the text? There surely was, and it gets more and more intriguing: they also found within this text the names of thirty-four of the most important Jewish religious teachers living in the last two thousand years. Every one was found, including their date of birth or death, in close proximity. The mathematicians calculated that the chances of this happening by accident were 775,000,000 to 1. On further investigation they found a lot more, including the name of God and the book title, all hidden within the text.

So what does this mean? What are the implications? In the context of our voyage of discovery it seems to speak of our intelligent designer at work here, embedding his signature in this most ancient of texts, to remain hidden until humanity had reached a certain level of technological advancement. For what reason? Perhaps to remind us that rather than making a god of science and technology we should look beyond the evidences around us to the cause of everything.

There are ghosts in our machines. These technological tokens of our cleverness are revealing things that would otherwise have remained hidden. The genie has been let out of the bottle and has grown far too complex to be allowed back in. Technological advances in the fields of astronomy, biochemistry and computer science have reopened the old debates between science and religion, and you can expect a fiery battle.

Notes

[1] Paul Davies, *Superforce: The Search for a Grand Unified Theory of Nature* (New York: Simon and Schuster, 1984), p. 243.

[2] George Greenstein, *The Symbiotic Universe* (New York: William Morrow, 1988), p. 27.

CHAPTER 8

FROM DAVID BECKHAM TO LITTLE GREEN MEN

The ball, hit with practised precision, spun through the chilly air, narrowly missing the left jug-ear of the burly defender, and buried itself in the top corner of the net. The crowd erupted, the team danced, the manager gyrated, the sponsors jostled for position and the scorer arched his back in triumph, spread his arms and breathed in the adulation. It's only a stupid game, cry the critics, ignoring the fact that football is now a billion-dollar business, that that goal would have been seen by millions worldwide and that the scenes of triumph would be repeated from ramshackle villages deep in the Congo to huge plasma screens in the heart of a Tokyo thoroughfare. For these people there is no direct benefit from the game beamed out from the heart of Europe, but the generated emotion is no less intense. David Beckham is an idol to millions, most of whom have no idea why. Is it his footballing skills? His boyish good looks? Or just the fact that his sponsors and marketing consultants have force-fed us all on his image?

The fact is that if it wasn't him it would be someone else. It's a pity that our generation reveres such flimsiness.

Our icons and idols are footballers, pop stars and film stars. Compare this with the 'pin-up boy' of two hundred years ago, Lord Nelson. Here was a true English hero. He scuppered the French at Trafalgar, leading from the front and dying a warrior's death. His funeral was arguably the grandest ever seen in this country and he is com-memor-ated to this day in Trafalgar Square. We need our heroes. They fulfil a need in us, a deep primeval need. It's a need to worship and it's as old as the ark. We say 'there must be something bigger and greater than myself' and we find ourselves worshipping gods of wood and stone: governments, gurus, or military, political and social leaders. The need to worship is one of the greatest needs of humanity. But David Beckham? It's a funny old world, isn't it?

Earlier societies didn't have the welfare state to look after their basic needs and had to feed themselves the best way they could, through hunting, fishing and farming. It wasn't easy. If an item that tickled their palate was out of season they couldn't just import it from else-where; they lived on a diet of whatever they could shoot, spear or coax out of the ground. Sometimes weather, competition from other humans or large animals, or other factors meant it wasn't even possible to do that. In those situations they either starved and died – or they got help from elsewhere. Enter the gods and goddesses of old. Hunters called on 'hunting' gods to guide their spears. Farmers called out to 'farming' gods and god-desses to ensure fertility of the soil. Other gods and god-desses were worshipped in the hope that they would help them in other ways, such as in childbearing and in matters of war. Other primitive societies, particularly in the Middle East, came to the realization that there was just one God who dealt with all of these matters and acted accordingly in a more efficient manner.

We don't have the needs of these ancient people. Our basic requirements of food, water, shelter and clothing are taken for granted, but we still have that aching gap inside – whether in our heart, in our guts, in our spirit or in our soul – that needs to be filled by something outside ourselves. In centuries past it was filled by an assortment of 'deities', from Jesus Christ to Allah, Buddha, Confucius and the large assortment of Hindu gods. These days, particularly for many in the West, traditional beliefs have been in decline, replaced by more tangible substitutes, from figures from the world of sport and showbiz on the one hand to theories and lifestyles such as evolution, consumerism, Marxism and the concoction of beliefs known as the New Age on the other.

There's a saying that goes something like this: 'When people stop believing in anything, they start believing in everything.' It's a fair description of life today. It used to be so straightforward. The majority of folk living in our country up to fifty years or so ago would have gone from the cradle to the grave claiming to be Christian. Their birth certificate and census forms would say 'Church of England' and that's how, if asked, they would have described themselves, even if they couldn't tell the difference between a parson and a parsnip. Now, thanks to a media overload, we're open to all sorts of ideas, lifestyles, philosophies, faiths and scams – or a combination of them all.

According to a recent survey conducted by the Science Museum in London, around 80 per cent of British people believe in aliens. Also about 6 per cent say that they believe they have seen a UFO, and half the people surveyed expressed an interest in experiencing life on another planet.[1] Concerning possible ambassadors for an alien encounter, Nelson Mandela was considered the best choice, followed by Patrick Moore.

Which brings me to my little green men. This was the favourite variety of aliens back in the 1950s, although these days, thanks to Steven Spielberg's ET, they are a little more greyish. They are all over the place, in movie blockbusters and TV mini-series; crazy people see them everywhere, others see them in unexpected places and scientists are falling over themselves to see them at all, or at least prove their existence.

For that last activity we can blame NASA, the National Aeronautics and Space Administration, in the USA. After a series of failures and disasters, the public was losing interest in outer space and NASA could see its multi-billion-dollar funding going down the toilet. They had to come up with something fast. In 1996 they did just that, when the head honcho declared that one of the key objectives was 'to search for Earth-like planets that may be habitable or inhabited through direct detection and spectroscopic measurement'.[2] They ramped up the interest when, two years later, they coined the new term astrobiology, the study of life in the universe. The lunatic fringe had now become mainstream and well funded.

But NASA wasn't the first scientific endeavour to concern itself with aliens and their ilk. In 1960, Dr Frank Drake, a radio astronomer, started looking for intelligent signals from outer space. He also developed an equation to calculate the number of civilizations that might exist in our galaxy. This became known as the Drake equation and was accepted by the scientific establishment. It stated that the number of civilizations in our galaxy whose radio emissions are detectable depends on the following:

- The rate of formation of suitable stars. (Can't have a planet without a sun.)

- The fraction of these stars with planets. (Can't have life without somewhere to put it.)
- The number of 'Earths' (i.e. habitable planets) per planetary system. (Can't put it where conditions aren't right.)
- The fraction of those planets where life develops. (Can't have ET without life developing.)
- The fraction of life sites where intelligence develops. (Can't make contact without the brains to figure out how to do it.)
- The fraction of those where technology develops. (No point having brains unless a good proportion of them take up science and technology as a career.)
- The 'lifetime' of communicating civilizations. (Needs to be some sort of overlap between our civilization and theirs, unless you want to miss them by a few billion years.)

Drake originally had only a single radio telescope to work with, but in the 1970s his work was continued by Zuckerman and Palmer, who had 384 of them, enabling them to keep a beady eye on a larger area of the night sky. Then, in 1984, SETI was born.

SETI, the Search for Extra Terrestrial Intelligence, was another initiative of Frank Drake. Although at one time it was partially funded by NASA, these days it relies on contributions from such as Paul Allen, one of the founders of Microsoft, and Steven Spielberg, still looking for ET's home planet. SETI is no part-time indulgence: its radio telescopes are able to monitor 28 million radio frequencies per second. If they're out there, surely SETI would root them out.

What they do is send a digital message containing something like the following: the numbers one to ten, the atomic numbers of the five elements essential to life on Earth, the chemical formula of the DNA molecule, the numbers for the average human height and the world's human population, as well as images of the human form and the Solar System (with Earth indicated as the planet of origin). This is deemed sufficient for any aliens to figure out that the signal is not a random jumble of impulses, but that a degree of intelligence is behind it and that this intelligence is keen to tell the aliens a bit about itself (nevertheless hoping that they don't decide to invade). More importantly, they monitor the noise of the universe, filtering out anything natural, mindful that anything remaining would be unnatural, produced by an intelligent brain with a grip on technology and born on an 'Earth-like' planet of a suitable star, where life had developed.

So how many civilizations have they found? Rest assured, if they had found anything we would have heard about it by now. So what's the point, and what would happen if they actually found something? Is it so important that we should find intelligent life out there?

Have you seen the irony of this search, in the light of our investigation of the benign conspiracy in the previous chapter? Millions of dollars are spent on telescopes to scan the heavens looking for signs of intelligence, yet in biology labs all over the world, microscopes see signs of intelligent design everywhere. So while the SETI chappies and others point their radio telescopes at the sky, looking for unnatural, non-random signals in a frantic search for intelligent life, others are investigating the DNA molecule, desperately trying to prove that its overwhelmingly unnatural non-randomness is in no way a product of intelligence.

There was a programme, *Alien Planet*, recently aired on the Discovery Channel. It was an expensively produced documentary in which a fictitious probe is sent to a far-off planet and we are shown a whole array of CGI-generated creatures living there, with commentary supplied by eminent scientists. It was all conjecture and fiction, of course, but clothed in respectability and kudos supplied by the scientists from NASA and the universities. It was basically a highly polished advert for both NASA and evolution. The planet was even named Darwin-4. One can only assume that the other three hadn't evolved decent enough CGI-animated monsters to make a good programme! Two quotes from this mockumentary are most telling. The clues are in the italics, supplied by me:

> 'If you look at the number of stars in the heavens (perhaps 10 billion trillion stars within range of our telescopes) and you realize that half of them *perhaps* have solar systems around them, and if you *play the odds*, you come up with the realization that *perhaps* there are billions of planets in our universe that have conditions that are compatible with life as we know it' (Professor Michio Kaku, City University of New York).

> 'I *think statistics* would say that life is a cosmic imperative' (Dr James Garvin, NASA).

It's all basically guesswork clothed in respectability, just as the stock market is pure gambling greed dressed in interesting suits and City addresses. These scientists don't know anything about life in the universe; they are just using statistics in the same way that you can get ridiculous odds against non-league Biffo Wanderers winning the FA Cup. You know that statistics won't give up the ghost and admit that for some things, there's going to be a zero chance of it happening.

Now can you see it? Scientists, funded by atheists, humanists and intellectuals, are trying to prove that we are not alone in the universe through a (so far) fruitless search for signals from the stars, while nature screams to us that we are *already* not alone, that an intelligent designer has littered our world with fingerprints.

Why do you think that people, when confronted with immediate mortal danger, often do something that years of sophistication, self-reliance and composure have not prepared them for? They cry out in desperation to a power outside themselves, whether to Mary the mother of God, Allah, or God himself. Eyewitness accounts of impending plane crashes and bomb scenes speak of a breakout of mass praying that would shame a Catholic Mass. When powerless, we invariably seek a power that may have the answers. It's an automatic reflex, it's natural; it's a spiritual hunger that is sharpened by the circumstances.

It all goes back to that need I outlined at the head of this chapter. We need to worship; there is a hole within us that can only be filled by our acknowledgement of something beyond us. Although we are reduced to filling it with David Beckham and little green men, there is something (or someone) else out there, at the heart of our benign conspiracy, knocking away at our hearts, asking to be let in.

Notes

1. Survey conducted as part of the exhibit, 'The Science of Aliens'.
2. In a speech given by NASA administrator Daniel S. Goldin at the 187th American Astronomical Society meeting in San Antonio, Texas, 17 January 1996.

CHAPTER 9

UNEXPECTED IMPOSSIBILITIES

By now you should be open to the possibility that there's something out there, even though you may be indifferent or even hostile to what or who it is. The story so far has presented you with hard facts and informed opinion. It's time to take things a stage further, to bring it to a personal level. It's time to ask the question: if there is a power out there interested in the affairs of human beings, how does that affect me? It's a fair comment that if there is an intelligent designer who has created us all and who is pulling the strings and guiding the destiny of the human race, why on earth would he or it be bothered with little old me or you?

After all, there are a few billion of us around, and surely the best use of time and energy would be to concentrate on the 'movers and shakers', the world leaders and policy makers, rather than butchers, bakers and candlestick makers. Or perhaps our intelligent designer has simply lit the blue touch paper and walked away. Perhaps his interest ended soon after he got the whole thing going, and he has now moved on to other, more interesting things in the cosmos at large. If this is true, there's no real hope for us, is there?

But the good news is that there's every evidence that this is not true, and I can give two reasons for that. First there's the evidence presented in previous chapters of this book, particularly when considering historical and present-day events. In those pages we witnessed a power that gave every indication of being interested in us mere mortals.

Secondly, there's what I would call personal testimony. There's a Michelangelo painting, 'God creates Adam', showing God reaching down and the man, Adam, stretching out his arm, with their fingertips about to touch. Contact is about to be made between the human race and an external entity, and it's very much one-to-one. Can an intelligent designer who created the snowdrop, the inner ear and the soccer hooligan be also interested in the personal comings and goings of billions of men, women and children? Let me tell you a true story.

A family I know had lived in the same house for many years and was desperate to move. The trouble was that financially it wasn't going to happen, and it seemed that they were going to have to stay put for some time.

Nine months later not only had they moved, but they had moved to the house of their dreams in an area they had always been desperate to move to. What had happened? Did they win the lottery or rob a bank? They did neither; they simply benefited from a series of unexpected impossibilities. Some would call them miracles, others would say coincidences. You will be the judge.

The story begins with another house, owned by the wife's mother. Once a family home, it was too large and high-maintenance for the mother, a widow, to continue to live in it. She wanted to sell. The trouble was that there were unruly squatters next door and nobody wanted to buy. An offer was made, subject to the removal of the squatters. But they had been there for years and seemed to be settled for good, as the house was owned by the Council, which was in no hurry to act on the matter.

The buyer was just about to pull out when, unexpectedly, the squatters were ejected and the house occupied by a bona fide family. The sale went through and then, immediately afterwards, this family was evicted and the house boarded up, a situation that would have deterred the buyer if it had happened just a week earlier.

A house then had to be found for the mother. If a satisfactory property could be found at a reasonable price, any money left over could be spent on their own house move. Meanwhile they had found their dream house, but the price was far beyond their budget.

The perfect place was found for the mother, a brand new property that had just been reduced by £55,000 for a quick sale, after the original purchaser had defaulted, losing his deposit. This was therefore an extra £55,000 in our friends' moving fund.

There were two major problems left. Firstly the dream house was a hot property, with many interested buyers, people who could afford the property. Secondly, our friends' own house was in a very poor state structurally and the best estimate still indicated a £50,000 shortfall on the amount need to buy the dream house, even taking the extra £55,000 into account.

Then an old friend, a trustee of a charity, came to visit. He had decided to look for a house in that very street just the week before! He liked the house and offered the full asking price, despite being given a survey report the size of a small telephone directory, with a catalogue of defects and blemishes that ought to have sent him running. On top of this, it was a private sale, so no estate agent fees had to be paid.

Back to the dream home. A phone call was made to the sellers. It appears that buyer after buyer had pulled out for a variety of reasons, so they were at the end of their tether and had dropped the price out of desperation just the day before. The sums now added up, and the dream house was within financial range. An offer was made and accepted.

The next day someone else made a higher offer but it was rejected. Why was it rejected? Well, the sellers' daughter had a dream the night before our friends visited, in which she was told that the house had to be sold to the next people to visit – our friends. The deal was completed and our friends finally moved, counting their miracles . . . literally.

Now this may seem a mundane story – after all, buying and selling a house is hardly exciting stuff, certainly not normally the stuff of miracles. But to our friends the whole episode, from start to finish, seemed to be orchestrated, as if they were really meant to make this move (even at the expense of the 'fall guys' of our little story – basically everyone else mentioned).

If you go through the story again you will find no less than six or seven unexpected impossibilities. One or two of them would have provoked a raised eyebrow, three or four would have produced mild incredulity, but six or seven?

I can vouch for this story because – surprise, surprise – it was *my* family and *my* mother-in-law, and the house is still our dream house.

A miracle is probably the most dramatic way our benign conspiracy can make itself known to you and me. It is defined as 'an event that appears inexplicable by the laws of nature and so is held to be supernatural in origin'. If our attention needed to be prodded in a big way, something inexplicable by the laws of nature seems a good place to start.

There was a man called George Muller. He lived in Bristol in the nineteenth century and had a heart for unwanted children. He decided to build orphanages to house these children, but all he had was 10p in his pocket. His miracle was that without once asking a single person for money, he received more than £1,400,000, allowing him to house and feed 2,000 orphans in five immense buildings. His was an incredible story and I urge you to read his autobiography.

Of course, not all miracles are financial. Most aren't, and if financial wealth could be guaranteed by prayer we'd all be millionaires by now. My son was healed one night of his veruccas, which was dramatic enough for us, particularly as he'd been plagued by them for years. Others have witnessed healings from cancer, AIDS and incurable diseases of all descriptions.

Now, unlike every other conspiracy you can think of, our benign conspiracy is not looking for secrecy, and although it works mainly in the background, that is not by choice. It's just that so few have been aware of it, particularly in this day and age. A conspiracy that, according to the thesis developed in this book, is responsible for life, the universe and everything has left its fingerprints everywhere. You don't need to be a forensic scientist to conclude that this suspect is not looking for secrecy. It wants to be known and acknowledged.

Imagine you were our intelligent designer. You've been trying for ages to grab the attention of the human race. You surrounded them with evidence of your design, you gave them beauty in nature, you even provided them with a conscience, yet they still don't, as a rule, acknowledge you. As they puff themselves up in their own cleverness, you are pushed further and further into the background. You become an irrelevance in their daily lives. This saddens you, but you don't give up. How do you grab their attention? Well, you shout at them! You act directly. You provide events that appear inexplicable by the laws of nature.

The problem is that not all 'miracles' come from our benign conspiracy; there's a lot of confusion out there. Take the 'miracle babies' of summer 2004, for example. An African preacher claimed that these were babies born without fathers, with some mothers churning them out every few months. There was, to say the least, controversy about whether these births really were a suspension of the laws of nature, but plenty of people wanted to believe they were miracles.

This type of story makes it harder for our benign conspiracy to grab our attention. If we witness a 'miracle' we are faced with three possibilities. It could be a fake, staged for human gain. This is the easiest option for our mind to grasp, as it comes from the safe world of human ambition and deceit. We can identify with this and can understand, though not condone, the motives. There's nothing scary going on here and, for many, all miracles would fall into this category, whatever evidence may be presented.

The second possibility is the most uncomfortable of all. This is when the miracle is authentic but its origin is in doubt. I realize that for many of you, the possibility of a benign conspiracy is difficult enough to swallow, but if I tell you that there is also a malign conspiracy out there that can perform its own miracles, that's surely enough to make you choke on your cornflakes.

There is no doubt that there is a supernatural world out there, the world of the unexplained, the Twilight Zone for real. It's the world of black magic and voodoo, of witches and spells. It can be an uncomfortable place and we're not going there with this little book.

The final possibility is the world where amazing things happen. It's where our benign conspiracy breaks through and announces itself in amazing ways. It's where people get healed of diseases, despite being written off by the doctors and experts. It's where people are rescued from life-threatening situations. It's even where an ordinary Joe can find his dream house. Above all it is where our intelligent designer speaks into our world, through miraculous deeds. It's not primarily so that people can be healed, delivered or helped. It's not just because he's a nice guy and wants to toss a few carrots out there to a few lucky recipients. A miracle is a signpost back to him, it's a scream from the hilltops, announcing that the creator of the universe wants to be known, to be acknowledged, to be loved.

This is mind-boggling if it is true. It speaks of goings-on in realms that most of us are totally unaware of as we travel through life. It speaks of an intelligent designer who wants to get personal, to be involved in our everyday lives.

CHAPTER 10

THAT STILL, SMALL VOICE

In 1942, at the height of the Second World War, a German reserve police battalion from Hamburg was given the mission of rounding up and massacring over thirty-eight thousand Jews in a village in Poland. The average age of these Germans was thirty-nine, they were middle-class, and most of them had no particular hatred of Jews. About a dozen out of the five hundred refused to take part and some more refused to carry on once the shooting had started, but the majority got on with it. Later on, some actually developed a liking for the job and actively volunteered to take part in death squads. They had acquired a taste for killing and it didn't concern them.

One of them said this: 'It was possible for me to shoot just the children. It so happened that the mothers led the children by the hand. My neighbour shot the mother and I shot the child, because I reasoned that the child couldn't live without its mother. This soothed my conscience.'[1]

They were just following orders. As one man subsequently admitted, it was not until years later that he began to consider that what he had done was not right. He had not given it a thought at the time.

Now, dear reader, you are not living under a restrictive military regime, where populations live their lives gripped by a cold fear, anxious to keep their heads down so as not to make waves and invite deadly repercussions. For that reason it is difficult for us to put ourselves in their shoes. Yet we must ask, would we have behaved in the same way as those ordinary Germans? Everything within my being wants to say no, these were evil people, from an evil race, who had chosen to live under such an evil regime. But the fact remains that they *were* ordinary people, living in such extreme circumstances that the simple matter of what is a right action and what is a wrong one had been muddled. Once free of this evil regime, these men were going to have to live with the facts and consequences of these actions for the rest of their lives.

So, how do we make decisions? It may seem an obvious question to ask, but why did these Germans live the rest of their lives in guilt, knowing that they had perpetrated such evil in the war years? Who or what told them at the time that they were doing right in killing those innocent Jews? Who or what told them later that they had done wrong? A defence could have been that they were following orders, but that's a cop-out, as some refused to join the killing squads without regard to the consequences. The majority carried out these deeds out of a sense of duty, yet years later they would be appalled at how they could have done so.

The answer to this mystery lies mainly at the feet of one man, Joseph Goebbels, the Nazi Propaganda Minister. His job was to justify Hitler's hatred of the Jews by convincing the German people that the Jews were a natural enemy of the German race and did not deserve to inhabit the same planet as them. As he had 100 per cent control of the official media, he had 100 per cent control over the information that filtered through to the German people, whether through radio, cinema, newspapers, cartoons, books, church sermons or drama. As Jewish books were burnt and prominent Jews (and their supporters) taken away from the public arena, the German people (in an age before the internet!) had no other input and so were liable to believe whatever hogwash Goebbels wanted them to believe. There were three main points that he hammered home unceasingly:

1. The Jews hate us. They provoked and brought about this war. What they mean to achieve by it is to destroy the German state and the nation. This plan must be frustrated and whatever treatment we give them is well deserved.
2. There is no difference between Jews. Every Jew is a sworn enemy of the German people and must be stopped at any cost.
3. Every German soldier's death in this war is the Jews' responsibility.

The ultimate aim of Goebbels (and Hitler) was to create such a negative picture of the Jew in the German psyche that every negative action against them could be justified, even the merciless killing of large numbers of Jews by death squads made up of ordinary Germans.

What Goebbels managed to do was to write a set of rules for the German people that would overwrite any others they had previously lived by. He had in fact replaced their conscience and was most proud of this. 'Conscience is nothing more than a crutch for cowards,' he proclaimed. This is in stark contrast to an earlier quote by Abraham Lincoln, who said, 'to sin by silence when they should protest makes cowards of men.'

So what is this conscience, a crutch for cowards or a condemner of cowards? Two opposing views and, to make an object out of the subject of our argument, we would say that one view was made by a man utterly without conscience and the other by a man governed by it. No wonder they said what they did.

It would be useful, at this point, to ponder what other people have had to say about the conscience:

'An individual who breaks a law that conscience tells him is unjust, and who willingly accepts the penalty of imprisonment in order to arouse the conscience of the community over its injustice, is in reality expressing the highest respect for the law' (Martin Luther King Jr).

'Never do anything against conscience even if the state demands it' (Albert Einstein).

'In matters of conscience, the law of majority has no place' (Mahatma Gandhi).

It is interesting to see that all three are saying the same thing and all three, in their particular spheres of influence, acted out their beliefs. Einstein was severely troubled by his conscience when, in later life, he saw the devastating consequences of his discoveries in atomic science. The conscience of both Gandhi and King led to a lifetime promoting non-violent protest and both were assassinated for their beliefs.

All of the above three were free thinkers who, although they came from three different religious and cultural traditions, were adamant that when it came to judging between what had become acceptable in society and what their conscience was telling them, conscience was to win every time.

So what is this conscience and how can it wield so much influence in our lives? Christopher Reeve, the actor who played Superman, said, 'I think we all have a little voice inside us that will guide us. It may be God, I don't know. But I think that if we shut out all the noise and clutter from our lives and listen to that voice, it will tell us the right thing to do.'

A little voice inside us? What little voice? Has it always been there? Were we just made that way? We need to think about this: don't they put away people who claim to hear voices?

This 'little voice' is the voice of your conscience and is considered the part of your mind which tells you whether what you are doing is right or wrong. We know all about it when we've done something wrong (e.g. stealing a friend's toy if you're a child, or stealing a friend's wife if you're an adult), because, assuming we are functioning correctly, we have a guilty conscience about the situation. It seems that the conscience's main job is to convict us of this guilt when we've 'transgressed', rather than commending us when we've been particularly good – that's when pride takes over and we start telling ourselves how wonderful we are!

As we found out, sometimes conscience can become confused or overruled. A member of a cult, or one of our 'ordinary Germans', would have been given a whole new set of values. They could be told that killing is good and compassion is a waste of time. Their conscience would thus be reprogrammed and a sense of right and wrong would be utterly distorted. We can then say that their consciences are seared, as they consider themselves to have a clear conscience to indulge in whatever acts they have been programmed to do, until, at some future time, they look back to reflect on their deeds.

So a conscience can be reprogrammed. But who programmed it in the first place? How does your conscience know what is right or wrong? Are our consciences taught to us? I believe that our conscience is as natural to us as our breathing. We are not taught to breathe – if we were, we'd all be dead before we reached the maternity hospital scales. In the same way, the organs of our body automatically go about their business from birth until they finally pack up a lifetime later. Even though we may teach our children to do good and live according to the laws of the land, the basic instinct is there already, with our conscience acting as our internal alarm to keep us on the right track.

As for where the conscience comes from, there are many theories and it all boils down to your particular world-view.

Conscience has been variously explained by philosophers. On one hand it could be a product of the senses, a kind of intuition, a product of one's feelings about what is right or wrong. On the other hand, some have said that it is a product of the mind, a conscious examination of what reason tells us is right or wrong. Others fall back on past experiences, suggesting that these can give direction to the choices made by an individual. Yet others, prompted by the ideas of Sigmund Freud, speak of the Superego, working in the background, in the unconscious mind. Other psychologists have identified conscience with an expression of values or guilt feelings, or as reactions to stimuli, external events.

All the above suggestions are introspective, speaking of the conscience as something that is developed by the individual, explaining it as a set of biological impulses in the brain and animal instincts.

The other alternative puts us fairly and squarely within our benign conspiracy, in a universe governed by an 'other'. In this scenario our conscience provides us with a connection to this conspiracy, a conduit between the natural world and the supernatural world. It's an invisible umbilical cord between us and something greater than ourselves. My contention is that our conscience is an identical filter built into all of us by an intelligent designer, to provide us with an absolute indicator of what is right and wrong. It's not a case of 'what's right for you' or 'I can see both sides in this case'. Instead you can see it as green and red LEDs deep inside you, lighting up either as 'yes' or 'no' for those important moral situations, where a decision is needed.

In all conscience, what you believe in is totally your choice. You have your own individual conscience, whatever you may believe about its origins. Tune in to your 'little voice' and listen to what it's telling you. Perhaps it will lead you to the same conclusion as mine.

Notes

[1] Christopher Browning, *Ordinary Men: Reserve Police Battalion 101 and the Final Solution in Poland* (London: Penguin Books, 2001), p. 73.

AND FINALLY

It is time to draw together all the strands and unmask the shadowy figure of our intelligent designer, to unveil the protagonist of our benign conspiracy.

There are said to be four candidates for our vacancy of intelligent designer, in a philosophical if not a practical sense. He could be a supernatural being, an extra-terrestrial, human, or God himself. I use three words for the first three options – dumb, dumber and dumbest – and put my money on the fourth one.

I won't insult your own intelligence by waffling about and trying to hide my intentions; it's already been too much of a strain. The fact is that we are looking at a *divine* conspiracy here and the intelligent designer is God himself, although, of course, we still need to ask the question, whose God?

All I have done is lay out the evidence, ask questions and challenge you to think for yourself, come to your own conclusions and, where you disagree, search further and see where that takes you – possibly to interesting, surprising and uncomfortable places.

One of the chief turn-offs about traditional religions is the sense of giving yourself over to a dogma set in stone and laid down by others, of switching off your brain and disengaging your common sense, allowing others to take over. My contention is that this has already happened.

What would you say if you discovered that your child was educated by teachers who were blindly following a belief system that is unproven and discredited by an increasing number of scientists, and who are influencing your child's thinking (whether they know it or not) in matters of religion, morality and science? The unavoidable fact is that evolution has, to all intents and purposes, become a religion. Since it is a system totally lacking in a supernatural, spiritual element, it is a place of safety for those who prefer not to believe in God. For these people, the alternative to evolution is unacceptable in ways that have nothing to do with science but are more to do with their personal preferences. Tell me one thing – is this an honest, mature way to think about the world around you?

Our benign conspiracy unfolded as we entered our journey of discovery in this small book. We heard about the Anthropic Principle, whereby it seemed that the universe had been put together solely for our benefit. The one who did this has been known as the intelligent designer, though some have been bold enough to develop this idea to its natural conclusion and give him the name of God.

Given that there is an entity out there who went to great lengths to fit together the divine jigsaw puzzle and to make our lives on Earth possible, this same entity is not just going to hang around and watch us blow it to smithereens, something that we are perfectly capable of doing in a variety of ways. So – and this is where we discern his benign nature – he decides to preserve us, to save us from ourselves. Why he does this we don't know, but we should be glad enough that he bothers about us.

Then we looked at life itself and explored the two possible alternatives – whether we evolved over millions of years from mould or whether we could have been designed and manufactured as a finished product, belly button and all. One aspect that we were urged to consider was information. Bearing in mind the amount of information needed by a computer programmer to get a piece of software to function, how much would be needed to run all the systems that make up our bodies – and where did it come from?

We then followed the usual arguments put forward in defence of the Theory of Evolution, to decide whether the goalposts have been moved since Charles Darwin's days by new evidence and scientific discoveries. We discovered that many who follow this theory are indeed nothing less than followers of a belief system, a faith that must be defended at all costs. George W. Bush himself has publicly stated that Intelligent Design is as likely an explanation as evolution for life and, in the USA at least, the controversy is being debated in some top universities.

Professor Richard Lewontin, an evolutionary geneticist, has said, 'We take the side of science in spite of the patent absurdity of some of its constructs. . . . It is not that the methods and institutions of science somehow compel us to accept a material explanation of the phenomenal world, but on the contrary, that we are forced by our a priori adherence to material causes to create an apparatus of investigation and a set of concepts that produce material explanations, no matter how counter-intuitive, no matter how mystifying to the uninitiated. Moreover, that materialism is absolute, for *we cannot allow a divine foot in the door*' (emphasis mine).[1]

And the high priest of Darwinism, Professor Richard Dawkins, asserts, 'I believe, but I cannot prove, that all life, all intelligence, all creativity and all "design" anywhere in the universe is the direct or indirect product of Darwinian natural selection (evolution).'[2]

Now tell me that evolution is not a faith!

The reason why the Theory of Evolution is so important to our secular materialistic society is that it is the main scientific 'prop' for the belief that there is no God. Kick that prop away and what do you have?

Then on to the history books, after sixty years of freedom bought at great cost by our forebears during the Second World War. Despite all the stories that came out of that conflict, little has been written of the miracles that preserved our nation at that time – until now. We looked at the National Days of Prayer announced by the King and wondered if it was just a coincidence that each was followed by unique and unexpected deliverances. If we think otherwise, we ask ourselves the question: which God were people praying to at that time?

Beauty was next on our agenda, and we were intrigued to discover how scientific it could be, thanks to the Divine Proportion. Rather than driving us to the bleakness of a mechanical universe, it suggests the hands of a master designer, creating rules and laws that bind together the structure of everything around us.

Technology and God are very unlikely bedfellows, but we discover that with the rise of new technologies we are able to view the world and the universe a little closer than ever before. What we can see is often most surprising, as we are now, for the first time, able to see the very fingerprints of God.

We also discovered that whatever we may think about our origins, we are born 'with a bit missing'. There's a hole inside us all that needs to be filled by something outside ourselves if we are to be made complete. Popular stopgaps these days range from David Beckham and his ilk to the little green men of outer space, but the intelligent designer had something else in mind, something at the very heart of the benign conspiracy – himself!

We walk about disconnected from our source, like ET stranded away from his home planet. We scramble around, desperate to satisfy this strange hunger. It's one of life's great sadnesses, particularly when our attempts seem to harm us rather than help us. God, our intelligent designer, is asking us to look at our designer labels and challenging us to follow the instructions in the small print.

Then we entered the world of the supernatural, the world of miracles. We saw this as a way that God can communicate directly with us. Although miracles can be great acts of healing or deliverance, their prime purpose is to point us to God himself, the great 'miracle man' in the sky.

We talked about this little voice within us, our conscience, and wondered where it came from and how it knows what actions are right or wrong for us. The reasonable view would be to accept that our conscience has been programmed into us by the intelligent designer, though we need to accept that not everyone would go along with this. Our challenge is to follow our own conscience on this one!

But a question was posed earlier: if God has revealed himself as the intelligent designer, then whose God is he? Who has got it right? Is he the God of the Jews, the Christians, the Moslems, the Hindus or the Buddhists? Could he even be the God of the Mormons, the JWs or the Scientologists? Could he be the God of all of them?

Well, it's a big subject. It's one thing to open you up to the possibility that God might actually exist, despite what the education system may have told you, but then to over-complicate matters by asking you to choose between a whole menagerie of gods, that's opening up a real can of worms.

Let me give you a hint. What do you do when you're looking for the phone number of John Smith? There are quite a lot of them about, so you want to be sure to get the right one straight away. You look up the name in the phone book, in on-line directories or through one of the 118 phone services. But the name's not enough: you need extra information in order to zero in on the one you're after. An address is good, something specific that can identify him without mistake. So you find your man and enjoy a nice phone conversation.

It's the same with God. There's a whole supermarket full of every variety of gods, powers, deities and supernatural entities. Just getting through to the first one you find is not good enough: you may end up communing with Molgoth, the red-eyed demon of the fiery furnace of Gwydnich. That certainly wouldn't do. You haven't come this far to get a wrong number in the divine directory.

So it's specific information you need. We need to get the right number, the first time. So what is it, this hotline to God, this link-up with the heart of the universe? Rather than give you God's address I will supply you with the credentials he himself provides for identification. It's quite simple. He is the God of the Bible, the divine author of that very book. It's his autobiography, the story of his life and his struggle. It's also a love story sweeping over many millennia, describing his often unrequited love for us, the human race. It sets down the problems, but also provides the solution. It's a big book, because it's a big story, and within its pages it provides the key to communicating with him.

First, it provides the names of the first people to whom he revealed himself in a significant way. They are Abraham, Isaac and Jacob and you will find them in the book of Genesis in the Bible, from chapter 12 onwards. You'll have to read the book yourself if you need to know more. You will find that God reveals himself in the Bible as the God of Abraham, Isaac and Jacob. That is his unique identifier. If you direct your inquiries to the God of Abraham, Isaac and Jacob, you're sure to get a first-time connection.

Secondly, and most importantly, he defines himself as the God who came to Earth in Jesus Christ and lived among us, died, then returned to life. You're an intelligent person and you're not going to take this bold assertion lying down, so I urge you to check it out for yourself. Of course, it may sound like a fairy tale, though it's pretty mild when you compare it with some of the stories coming from the 'I met an alien' camp. But again, check the facts for yourself and don't just file this away with the assorted legends, sagas and fantasies that have assaulted our minds over the years.

Seriously, and finally, this God is the real thing, the perfect fit for the hole in your heart, because he put it there to start with when he created you. But don't just take my word for it; contact him, using the credentials I have given. He'll never be engaged and although you may not think you're getting an immediate connection, he'll always get back to you.

Why not give it a try and learn about the divine conspiracy first-hand?

Notes

1 Richard Lewontin, 'Billions and billions of demons', *The New York Review*, 9 January 1997, p. 31.
2 The quote was Richard Dawkins' response to a question posed to one hundred and seventeen scientists and others by John Brockman, publisher of *The Edge*, a science website, on 4 January 2005.

RECOMMENDED READING

This is only a small book tackling big subjects. It doesn't have all the answers; it just poses a few questions. Some questions are not easily answerable, but a look at the following is as good a place to start as any.

Chapter 1: Starry, Starry Night
Gonzales, Guillermo and Jay Richards, *The Privileged Planet*, Regnery, 2004

Chapter 2: The End is Nigh
Website *Exit Mundi*, http://www.exitmundi.nl

Chapter 3: Life, Just as We Know it
Burgess, Stuart, *Hallmarks of Design*, Day One, 2000

Chapter 4: It's All in the Design
Gillen, Sherwin, Knowles, *The Human Body: An Intelligent Design*, CRS Books, 2001

Chapter 5: Our Darkest Hour
Gardner, David, *The Trumpet Sounds for Britain*, CFP, 1983

Chapter 6: The Eye of the Beholder
Livio, Mario, *The Accelerating Universe*, Wiley, 2000

Chapter 7: Ghosts in the Machine
Behe, Michael, *Darwin's Black Box*, Simon & Schuster 2003

Chapter 8: From David Beckham to Little Green Men
Bates, Gary, *Alien Intrusion*, Master Books, 2004

Chapter 9: Unexpected Impossibilities
Muller, George, *The Autobiography of George Muller*, Whitaker House, 1984

Chapter 10: That Still, Small Voice
Strobel, Lee, *The Case for a Creator*, Zondervan, 2004